the
brink
a memoir

JAIME ANDREWS

ISBN: 979-8-9877403-0-9 (pbk)
ISBN: 979-8-9877403-1-6 (ebook)

"The man who writes about himself and his own time is the only man who writes about all people and all time."

— George Bernard Shaw

"Also, women."

— Jaime Andrews

PREFACE

I barely recognize the person to whom you are about to be introduced. You may not like her, but that's fair, because she didn't like herself very much either. Yes, "she" is me, but she also couldn't be further from the person I am now. I am so sorry for the people she hurt with her actions, and for those she may hurt with the words found herein. With gratitude to my mother and sister - neither of whom will read this - but who are responsible for me finding myself again. Just know…it takes a second book.

ONE

The desk I am sitting at says that I am a slut. Not as a self-declarative, but actually using my name. Huh. I wonder if the chick that wrote it knows that I sit here. It's obviously a chick. It's obvious, not just from the swirly and bubble-bedecked handwriting, but also because guys tend to be more appreciative of that sort of thing. What are the chances that I should sit at the one desk in this school that says something awful about me? Maybe there are more of them. Maybe they all say it.

I consider writing in retort, "No, she's just misunderstood," or "lonely" or "sad" or "lacks self-control while under the influence, for God's sake," but I can't fight anymore. Besides, sticking up for yourself in third person seems pretty lame.

The next day, I find that someone has done the job for me. It says that I'm nice. I can't imagine who this benevolent defender could be, considering that I don't have many friends. The friends that I do have would probably agree with the initial statement. Heck, one of them might have written it. The exchange goes back and forth for a couple of days with a third party finally interjecting an emphatic testament to my whoredom, which seems to silence all. It's funny that I'm not running to class every day to see what is said of me next. My head is an observation balloon. I'm numb.

I'm 14 now, in my first year of high school. I can map out

exactly how it got to this point, but am not particularly cognizant of why. Let me begin at the beginning: I'd had an impossible standard set for me at birth when my mother cooed, "She's perfect," upon first seeing me. True, she was on lots of drugs at the time. Funny how much better things can look that way.

I was born on a Thursday. I often think of that old adage, which claims "Thursday's child has far to go." When I hear concepts that make sense to me, I am haunted by them. I debate whether being Thursday's child means that I will go far, or that I have a lot to learn and it will be a long road. I had always imagined it would be the former, but it is certainly looking like I'm going down the latter.

My parents don't love each other. Okay, they don't even really like each other. It's my mom's second marriage and, to be sure, it is one of convenience. She didn't think anyone else would have her, what with a young daughter from a rocky three years with her high school sweetheart. Mom's first love came back from Vietnam all pot and parties. When my dad came along - her boss at the bank, from a good family, socially inept - he must've looked like salvation.

Dad worked a lot. He also spent a lot of time in the basement. I believe that he was forging a special relationship with a certain illicit cable network. Often when descending the stairs to his lair, the sounds of soft sighs and saxophones would abruptly shift to the roar of a stadium and the bleating of some cocky sportscaster. I used to have nightmares about the basement. Some demonic force like a figure made of red-hot wrought iron would be coming toward me slowly and I was unable to run. I guess everyone has dreams like that, but these dreams, coupled with the knots like ghoulish faces in the fake wood basement paneling, always propelled me up the stairs at a dangerously fast pace. Sometimes I would dream that the stairs were gone entirely, and there was no escape.

Everything from my preadolescent years is kind of hazy, which is funny because it's the stuff that followed I'd prefer to forget. I've been told that I used to hurl myself over the bars of my crib and on to the floor. My parents would be woken by a thud in the middle of the night just to find me on my girly-pink carpet, staring up at them. Nine months old and already looking for a way out. Once my mother said they were meeting with an insurance agent in the living room while I was screaming and tossing myself against the walls. She said it sounded like I was being tortured, but they went on with their meeting as though nothing were happening. It's called Ferberizing. Your parents are supposed to just let you freak out alone. "Is she all right in there?" the agent apparently asked. They told him to ignore me. They certainly did.

My revisionist history speaks of a happy childhood, but the second hand reports seem to belie that. I was precocious and petulant, given to tantrums and willful misanthropy. On a trip to the pet store, the killie-shiller asked if I wanted a pretty fish. I said I wanted an ugly one. When people asked if my favorite color was red or pink? I would say it was black. I was no more than four. Maybe I was just rebelling against what was to come. My favorite movie was "Watership Down." You know, the cartoon with all the dying bunnies? I watched it over and over and over again. I planned a performance of it in our backyard. I didn't follow through, though. Nobody else was interested. This would be a recurring theme.

Our family meals, generally a rotating repertory of the easy-bake variety, were invariably held in front of the television set. My father would eat his reheated portion alone in the basement when he finally returned home from a day of work in the city. I hadn't been conscious of being resentful of his consistently subterranean state, but I must have been. I know this because one Sunday morning when Mom, my sister Carrie and I were going to church, I turned the lock on the basement door before leaving.

As we pulled out of the driveway, our lamppost flickered. My mom said she would have Dad look at it, but I was pretty sure that he was doing just that. I was particularly exultant that day at First Presbyterian. I knew we would be going out to lunch afterward too. We always did.

Dad was pretty infuriated when we finally got home, particularly because we hadn't recognized the lamplight's flicker as Morse code for SOS. There were no sailors amongst the women of my household, it seemed. I'm sure I was scolded, I'm sure I said it was an accident, and furthermore, I'm sure my sister and I laughed about it afterwards. As angry as dad was, it was hard to take him seriously. His rage was impotent because it was omnipresent. Dad would bristle if you weren't pouring your cereal out right or if the door closed too loudly. When someone is mad all the time it's hard not to find it funny. You have to laugh as your nerves are fraying.

My mom felt guilty for staying with him so long, but it's not her fault. My dad puts up a pretty good front and it's easy to dismiss men's quirks, particularly when they mirror your own father's. Pop-pop had the capacity to make my dad look downright warm. Plus, there was "staying together for the kids," a phenomenon which I'm fairly certain does more harm than good.

My mom has told me that dad's behavior didn't seem to faze me when I was little, that I just ignored him. She knew it bothered Carrie, though. It must have been hard for my sister. Her real dad was gone. He had tried to be partier and parent but my mom wouldn't stand for both and he opted for the former. So poor Carrie found herself a flower girl at four, heralding the welcome of this cruel alien into her life. Then, just over a year later, my arrival forced her into the big sister role. Dad could be ever so slightly more forgiving with his own spawn, but he had less patience for that which he had not created. When she grew older and heavier under his scrutinizing eye, he would compound her self-loathing with a "Carrie, don't eat these" post-it on his potato chips. So, you can't blame me when I agreed to say that I had eaten 2 of the 4 missing cupcakes, for example. She was my sister. She was beautiful and terrifying. I wouldn't even tell anyone when I heard her retching in the bathroom later on. I didn't even know what that meant.

Carrie had no trouble manipulating me. 5 1/2 years my senior, my little button face must've seemed an easy to push emblem of our mother's disastrous union. She was able to con me out of the larger bedroom by telling me she had seen spiders in there. She was willing to switch with me because, see, she wasn't afraid of spiders. I didn't even realize I'd been duped until years later, by which time I believed she deserved the larger room by virtue of her chronological superiority, if not her utter savvy in the realm of child psychology.

I'm sure it was fun to torture me, really. I was probably even more of an exposed nerve than I am now and the thrill has still not worn off for legions of my peers. Having me around the house must have been tantamount to your very own personal, poke-able Pagliacci, a cartoon puppy to kick around. Heck, Carrie would even invite her friends over to get in on the action. Her best friend Lisa would stand before me in the kitchen and say, "Jaime, I love you," before turning sharp an instant later and sneering, "Jaime, I hate you." She would go back and forth like that as my face rose and fell with every reversal, and then contorted with confusion and tears.

And I don't mean to be all victimy here - "Poor me," and all that - Carrie and I really got along. I mean, I gather that other stuff's just normal sibling shit.

Our senses of humor and self were similarly warped and we spent a lot of time laughing uncontrollably at jokes nobody else would understand. At one point we even proposed building a communication window between our rooms. Okay, that was my idea…come to think of it, my sister probably counted on it being denied. There aren't too many parents keen on putting holes in their walls at the request of their children. It was nice of Carrie to humor me though.

Of course, she also smacked my face so hard once that a handprint of broken blood vessels stained my cheek. She told me to explain the mark to my mother by saying I'd walked into a door. When the flags as red as my face went up at school the next day, I was summoned to the school nurse. She asked me with concerned eyes what had happened, and my typical-of-abuse excuse prompted a call home. Mom verified the tale of my clumsiness because as far as she knew, I had, in fact, walked into a door.

TWO

It's funny that the administration of Seamen Neck Elementary School – yes, Seamen Neck – was so concerned about my well-being, seeing as how they exhibited little of this concern while I was actually under their care. On an almost daily basis, I was sent to the nurses' office following an incident with one Gianni Giancoli. How the in-school beatings of a very small girl by a rather prematurely large boy were allowed to continue, I'll never know. If it's true that such violent behavior is an expression of a young boy's affection, then Gianni must have liked me an awful lot. I would say that there was a huge hole in that theory if it hadn't borne the cliché "you always hurt the one you love." Clichés have to be true or they never would've gotten that way.

My yen for retaliation was not out of love. For weeks I saved my Flintstones' vitamins with the grand plan of taking them all in one day, consequently garnering the superhuman-strength to pummel my foe. It worked too. That day, at recess, I straddled Gianni in the schoolyard and flailed at his face, which he fought to block as he cried. Back in the classroom, Mrs. Romanoff cheered my name, along with the other students who surrounded us.

I think this may have been a dream. If it were reality, I'm fairly certain I'd not have seen my teacher cheering from her desk. It was pretty vivid though, and I derive pride from it nonetheless. Meanwhile, in reality, my head was being slammed so hard into our wooden cubbies that my mom said I was coming home with eggs on my head. The last of these lumps was so Grade-A large that my mother finally called Gianni's parents.

After his torture was exposed, Gianni would give me money instead of contusions. I'm not sure where he got the payoff cash, though the Giancolis clearly had a bit of money. Theirs was the glowing, animatronic-laden house people drove for miles to see around Christmas time. When mom found the cash, she - knowing I hadn't an after-kindergarten job - made me return it. I resented this, thinking the money only fair restitution for my pain and suffering. Were we litigious, I could have gotten a lot more. People didn't do stuff like that then, suing for every little thing. We weren't that kind of family, anyway, however I might have wished we were.

Resentment was already making a strong showing in my ever-so-young palate of newfound emotions. As crayon drawings of our families were returned to us I noticed that John Fozzio, who resided across the way from me in class as he did on Sylvia Lane, had a gold star on his paper precisely like the one I had, despite the fact that his drawing was clearly inferior to my own. I brought them both to Mrs. Romanoff and pointed out the discrepancy of product in relation to the similarity of reward. She explained to me that my drawing was good for what I could do and John's was good for his apparently diminished capabilities. After all the kid had been born with an extra finger and, lest you think young lisping John a miracle, you should know that the finger betwixt his thumb and pointer was as useless as it was boneless, and was more likely a result of his loud, scary mother's chain smoking than any marvel of evolution.

I was not yet prepared to accept our society's glorification of mediocrity and balked against the communist line of the classroom, reasoning that if something is better it deserves corresponding praise. She called my mother to remark how strange it was that I'd done such a thing. Though my mother understood my motivation, Mrs. Romanoff thought my question highly unusual and deserving of some sort of reprimand. Maybe that's why she let me get beat up so much, to take me down a notch.

I know it's gross, but I always thought that I was special. Different. I was a natural leader - or more likely, "bossy" - but only because I was sure that my ideas were better. I never pointed this out to friends, I simply enforced my will. Playtime at my house meant improvisational games, playwriting, poetry and architecture. Yes, architecture. We would draw our dream homes, 6-story behemoths with amusement parks on the top floor. Not likely to be structurally sound, but something to work toward, nonetheless. We would also plan our dream weddings.

My love for all things penis-bearing reared its head early on. I chased Lyle Caruthers around the classroom and declared him my boyfriend. If only men remained forever that easy. Actually, come to think of it, in that year's class picture he is leaning rather precipitously toward this cute blonde. I guess I should've paid closer attention to her moving in on my toddler turf.

Oh-so-sadly, she of the flaxen locks moved by the end of the year - and not a lick too soon either as she had been cast as the lead in the kindergarten play. See, my performance yen was also in full effect by this time. I'm sure it had nothing to do with needing attention. No, I had something to communicate! I was thusly called upon to tackle a dual role in "Millions of Cats," a lovely tale in which the eponymous felines present themselves to a prospective master and, in their competition, wind up clawing each other to death, leaving only "the loneliest little kitten."

That's a pretty dark show for kindergarten, and it thusly appealed to my sensibilities. So, I got to be a Siamese cat (which were totally my favorite) as well as the loneliest little kitten, the one who is eventually adopted due to an apparent pacifism that kept him out of the fray. I have no idea if I pitched a fit to have these roles bestowed upon me or whether they just were.

My mom always makes a big deal out of the fact that I got to name the gerbils in first grade. Had I been assigned the task or had I just adamantly rejected the other options and asserted the superiority of the names I had chosen? I think the latter is possible. My sister got a Yorkshire terrier at about this time and I stewed that the name "Samantha" was chosen. That was no kind of DOG'S name. Not to be out-gifted, the dog doling resulted in me getting gerbils of my own, progeny of the class rodents. Being white and brown, I named them Sugar & Cupcake, not exactly boundary-breaking in terms of childhood pet names.

Anyway, Lyle and I remained an item, though by the following year he had grown prematurely awkward. I moved on, but not before baring my pointless little body to him after a swim in the pool one day. For some reason I had coerced his little sister to join me in the flashing. This is more disturbing in retrospect. I had a bit of an exhibitionist streak going. Following a shower one day at home, I stood naked on the window ledge of my room facing the street. I implore any psych majors to offer their hypotheses in this regard.

Carrie and I were kind of over-sexualized. Mom used to tell us salty jokes early on, and her and my sister both would make fun of my tiny little behind.

Once they burst through the unlocked bathroom door and took pictures of me in the shower that came out as all crouching body and big, wet, shocked head. Pictures like that coming through a Fotomat would put child protective services on high alert nowadays. Do parents still take naked pictures of their children? They did seem to take it pretty seriously at summer camp when I tried to pull the same shit on a whiny little camper girl in the locker room. The shocked and dismayed administration took my film and called my mother to come and pick me up. She couldn't very well yell at me considering she was the one from whom I'd learned the technique.

But back to first grade, where a new enemy was born in the pale and paunchy person of Aaron Lubble. He competed with me at every opportunity. He probably imagined he had thought up better gerbil names, and was likely real pissed when I was given the titular role in the Mrs. Malinski production of the Little Red Hen. C'mon, I had experience! Okay, I was to share the role with Dana Strong, but I did get to take the reins entirely when she puked at dress rehearsal.

Things with Aaron came to a head later in the year when I started a class newspaper. I told you that I was annoying. As editor-in-chief and head reporter, I was dealt the unfortunate card of having to let Aaron go following creative differences. Something concerning the masthead, I believe.

He immediately started his own publication and we devolved to sadly sexually segregated staffs. Though neither of us was ever official enough to say, go to print, Aaron and I each had badges proclaiming our multitudinous titles taped to the corners of our desks. Each day, the two of us became more and more multi-hyphenate, attempting to best each other with the scope of our respective positions. By the time my placard proclaimed involvement in every aspect of publishing that I could fathom, it was half past the boiling point and Aaron, en route from the bathroom, ripped from my desk the symbol of my leadership. I sprung from my chair and removed his as well. A fairly weak retaliatory gesture I grant you, but I saw no reason to escalate at this point, not that I would've known how to do so.

A chase ensued and I ended up with my back bent over the radiator, my shoulders being pushed down by Aaron. I have no idea where Mrs. Malinski was, I saw only fury. I charged at my attacker, driving him across the room. Near the blackboard, my nauseous new compatriot Dana grabbed and held him fast. She was a big girl. I sunk my teeth into the porcine flesh of his right upper arm and he squealed, as could be expected. I was a rabid beast. I was snarling. I drew blood.

Although a discussion was had with the principal, the reprimand ended there. I had gotten away with it. I maintain that the powers that be had decided Aaron deserved the wound he received and that, myself blameless, no parental intervention was required. I breathed the heaviest sigh of relief a seven-year-old can muster. All seemed well until the sunny afternoon 3 days later when Mrs. Lubble approached mom's brown Chevy station wagon after school, Aaron in tow. I squirmed in the passenger seat with the blood pressure I didn't know I had rising. She yanked up his sleeve exposing the still ruby mark of my incisors and the surrounding purple bruise. "Look what your daughter did to my son."

Because future chiropractic bills were not at my disposal, I had no physical proof of the injury that had preceded my violence. I was punished for a week, my longest stint ever, and cried the whole time. My arguments of injustice went unheard, as any attempt to reason this out with my mother was met with the oft-heard admonishment not to be "fresh." As usual, my request for clarification of this term only got me in further trouble, although I really did just want an explanation. Fresh sounded like a good thing to me. Works for food, right?

THREE

Shortly after being released from captivity, I was playing with my best friend Myra from across the street. She was older sister to my classmate John of the extra digit and inferior drawing. Her bulb glowed no brighter than his, though, true, she had no scar where a floppy finger once dwelt. As we played -- likely with Barbies, and likely mashing their naked plastic bodies together in some hypothesized sexual act -- my sister told us she was going into the shower. While the water ran in the bathroom, the doorbell rang.

When I opened the door, I found Carrie oddly dressed and be-wigged, claiming to be the Avon lady and asking for my mother. Now, I called her on it, "Very funny, Carrie" and all that, but her insistence and feigned confusion made me question myself. Maybe this WAS the Avon lady after all.

"She's not here," I said.

"Well, can I come in and wait for her?"

"No, come on, Carrie."

"Who is Carrie?"

"C'mon. You know. My sister. Come on."

"Well, perhaps she would be interested in Avon's products, may I speak with her?"

"C'mon, Carrie. No, she's in the shower," I was stammering. My youth allowed me to accept both realities. Her jaw clenched. "Just let me in." She swung the screen door open and brandished a foot-long knife, the kind you're scared of even when it's just sitting in the drawer. Screaming, I ran into my room and closed the door, a fairly useless deterrent considering the lack of lock. I pulled Myra with me under the bed as Carrie or the Avon lady or this psychotic killer slowly opened my door. If she said anything, we couldn't hear it over our own piercing, small-girl screams. The blade of the knife was thrust and jabbed under the bed. It moved from side to side as we tried to press ourselves through the rear wall. Then it stopped. We weren't injured. She just went away.

When we finally felt safe enough to leave our shelter, the water from the shower turned off and my sister emerged from the bathroom wrapped in towels. "Were you guys screaming?" she asked. I told her that I hated her. When my mother got home, I wasted no time in telling her of my torment at Carrie's hands. Her defense? It was Friday the 13th or April Fool's Day or something. Either way, it was convincing enough that Carrie went out that night. I suppose my mother figured she deserved no more punishment than life in this house already afforded her, but I was furious that she suffered no repercussions. It seemed you only got time in this house if you drew blood. I kept hoping that Myra's mother would come by three days later and show my mom the scar that my sister had left on her daughter's brain.

A couple of weeks later, on Easter, my gerbils committed suicide. Now, you can argue that rodents are not capable of such decisions, but what would you call it? They wadded cedar shavings under their wheel thing so that they could climb up it to the top of the cage. Then they hurled themselves out and onto the floor. Okay, it was more likely an attempt at escape, but seeing as how it resulted in the breaking of Sugar and Cupcake's neck and spine, respectively, I'm inclined to take a darker view. I cried all day until I was offered my choice of gerbil or hamster replacements. This was unwise, as surely my parents knew that Sugar and Cupcake were likely trying to escape the rather meager food rations that I only sporadically remembered to dole out to them.

Or, perhaps, they were trying to flee from the next time I was going to set them in the holes of the pool table and roll balls after them. Still, the gerbils were replaced by hamsters, whose demise I don't recall. I'm fairly certain the causes were as natural as they can be for animals subjected to such torments. I do, however, know that the resultant replacement gerbils bred and took to eating their young, a sight so horrifying that I was pretty much cured of any further desire to care for rodents. Damn shame too, because putting those things on the record player and watching them revolve slowly, then turning up the speed until they flung off, was a pleasure not to be missed. I fancied myself an animal lover.

FOUR

The only remarkable thing that I remember about 2nd grade was that my teacher was named Mrs. Butz, which is a terrible name if you're going to be teaching 2nd grade. There were rumors about the 3rd Grade teachers. Everyone feared getting Mr. Bellingdon, who apparently had a predilection for chair throwing. At the year's close, he cornered two of my friends and me in the hallway and asked us whom we wanted as our teacher the following year. We stammered and stared. We knew only that we didn't want him, and he knew that. He watched us squirm. Using up my lifetime supply of Zen before hitting ten, I answered, "Well, I don't have any control over it, so I'll be happy with whoever I get." When I told my mother that, she was very proud of me, and I was very proud that she was very proud.

When I finally got to 3rd grade, though, my mom had started working full time again at another bank. I had to take classes after school to fill up the time before she got home. One class was cheerleading. Oh, how I wanted to be a cheerleader. They were hot and boys liked them. I wanted to b-e aggressive. I also took creative writing. Unfortunately, however, our assignment to create a newspaper wrought another call home with my lead story, "Man Falls from Sky Believed to be God" - complete with illustration. I thought it was hysterical, but apparently the folks in charge were not ones for satire and deemed it "disturbing and wildly inappropriate." Nobody ever talked with me about it. I just heard the murmurings.

What the powers that be were doing with all this data of my deviance is beyond me. Someone evidently thought my powers should be trained for good, and I was brought into the "Gifted and Talented" program, which essentially meant that I got to leave class to build circuits and do brain teasers. There I was, feeling special again.

I joined the school band as a French horn player. I hadn't so much chosen it as I had its greatness thrust upon me simply because I was the only one to express even mild curiosity beyond the flute and clarinet. I think the most impressive thing about my horn career was that, in carrying it, I doubled my mass.

I was also a tiny dancer. Pretty good at it too until puberty rendered me all gangly limbs and misfiring coordination. I'd started in kindergarten, and performed in the recital despite a large knee bandage, a result of my first set of stitches.

Larry and Robert Inglese, the neighbor boys, were at my house, playing with marbles in the basement. What do kids even do with marbles besides roll them around, I'm not sure, but they were scattered all over the floor. When it was time for them to leave, we darted about to pick them up. I knelt to retrieve one and was pierced by pain. I ran up the stairs with my hand over my gushing knee, crying like crazy. My parents were pretty desensitized to this sound emanating from me, and didn't take it seriously until I removed my hand to reveal the geyser. Dad said he'd go get a band-aid and mom said he was an idiot. Clearly, I needed to go to the hospital. It was only four stitches, but the gauze was enough to make my recital pictures depict me as quite the little trooper.

Future recital footage betrayed a penchant for comedy that I wish I'd adhered to rather than the drama I seemed to perpetuate. While dancing as little Mae Wests to "Let Me Entertain You," I stepped with my left whilst others stepped with their right and made a guilty face to rival Stan Laurel. The crowd went wild. Well, they laughed, anyway.

When a neighbor-lady was doing my make-up in preparation for the show, dad had walked up with his camcorder to film the act for posterity. I sensed his approach and turned to the camera shocked, then giggled, turning back to my preparer and saying, "What's HE doing here?" Comedy magic, I tell you.

This unreserved distaste for my father made frequent appearances. Were they my feelings or simply ones transferred to me by the elder women of my clan? I'm not sure. I certainly had enough of my own reasons to find fault with him. Dad would make promises that he didn't keep, and had an endless stream of excuses why. He showed little interest in performing any family-related tasks, the least of which was dinner. Even at functions held by his own side of the family, dad would slink away to lie down for a while. Life seemed to exhaust him so. Parties held by my mother's family he would not bother to attend at all. Plus, dad was the one to dole out the corporal punishment.

I wasn't spanked often, but the execution was more impactful than the frequency. Dad's face would contort in a mask of furious passion. Rage came off him in waves. He didn't spank Carrie. He didn't dare, he wasn't her real father. I think that sometimes I bore the brunt of an attack meant for the both of us. It enraged him that she stoked my anti-father fire, and once, as we sat watching TV, refusing to listen to him, he pulled me into my room by an arm and leg. As he hovered over me on my bed, I screamed for him to hit me harder, that it didn't hurt. When he came to talk to me later, poking his head around my door, I closed it. He screamed as I pressed his head between the door and its frame and pressed with all the weight of my minor personhood. He lay down for the next two days, claiming he had a headache. Like I was supposed to feel badly for what I had done. He was such a baby.

Carrie and I found the "Penthouse" magazines in Dad's drawer. We stared at the plastic perfection of the women inside with mingled awe and disgust. Who was this creepy man living in the basement and looking at these girls? The anti-dad sentiment in the house ran pretty high. There was a constant front. I just kind of checked out.

FIVE

A 4th grade trip to see "Cats" struck me, perhaps too hard. I danced alone in the basement to its nerdy-ass score until my everyday movements were feline. I recruited friends to join me in my bestial celebration and, before I knew it, we had a couple of hours-worth of class time to arrange the desks around the periphery and show our peers a little of our free form interpretation. I can't imagine how this came about and why it was agreed to. Maybe all the teachers ran off to get wasted together for a while. Really, I should've been stopped. Students from other classes were trotted in to see what we were doing and I'm not even sure what that was, nothing more than crawling around on overturned desks, really. I am sorry in retrospect for subjecting my peers to my rampant egotism, though at the time, of course, I thought it was pretty brilliant. When my good old adversary Lubble made it into the room and balked at the sheer lameness of the spectacle, I crawled to a desk and, facing him while standing on it, I raised my left leg over my head with my hand. I glared at him while holding the pose interminably, as though silencing him with the sheer marvel of my physical capacity.

I realize now that I was intolerably obnoxious. I was at the center of things and needed to be there. In the year of the "Cats", I sat on a desk flanked by some girls and announced that I had to go to the bathroom, so certain was I that I had gotten my first period. I was obsessed with maturity, sexuality, having breasts. I was convinced that my boyish frame was already sporting a pair of them. The only thing that was getting big for me was my britches. The setbacks rattled me.

I got my first C in a lifelong series of A's due to being disruptive with my chatter, rather than as a result of any inferior performance. It wasn't really fair, especially because she gave me the C in English, which was my favorite. Math I would've understood. I was a little slower on the times tables than other kids. My mind would seize, uncertain. It happened a lot.

I was the only 4th grader asked to do a solo on "Somewhere Over the Rainbow" with a group of 5th graders for the Winter Concert. I made it through the daytime performance, but like my friend Dana before me, I had thrown up beforehand. I didn't let it stop me the way she did, though, nobody even knew. The show must blah blah, right? But at night, before all the parents and all my peers, I forgot all the words I was supposed to be singing. Now, give me a break, it was an obscure verse, not that 'way up high' crap that everyone knows. The other girls turned to me suggesting lines but they were wrong. I didn't know what was right and so I didn't say anything. Adrenaline shot up to my face, burning it, and when the song ended, I skulked out in tears. Boy, did Lubble have a field day with that one. At least once daily he would approach me and start singing "Somewhere over the --", then devolve into a choking noise.

I attempted to save face at the spring concert by wrangling 7 minutes to perform a fully choreographed medley from "Cats," complete with garbage cans and overuse of the dance move, "The Snake." However, when we made a last-minute change that little Abby Bennett failed to implement in performance, the show closed with us having a screaming match as we exited. Mom was horrified, but I think it was funny. Well, it was funny in retrospect, anyway, especially considering I wasn't the one who was wrong. Still, I hated to have mom disappointed in me.

SIX

I started feeling everything so intensely. The song "I wear my sunglasses at night" was on the radio in the carpool from dance class and my head felt like it was going to explode. It really is a stupid song.

One day I pounded my skull against the school's brick-face wall when I was once again neglected by my then love Joey Kessler. I tried to chalk it up to him not liking girls yet, for surely there was no other reason to spurn me, but then, as now, I was probably a bit too much energy to accept.

At Lee Elwin's birthday party - the first coed one that I recall having sexual implications - Joey was carried toward me screaming all the while. I sat there smug and waved my hands, welcoming. What was I, 9 years old? Jesus. Through scrambling and flailing, he never made it to me. Things were changing at that party. The small group there - less than ten of them - turned on me. They attacked my good grades, my penchant for forcing people to watch me dance to widely reviled show tunes. Soon it was Lindsay Tannenbaum from down the block, she with whom I used to dance to the "Flashdance" soundtrack, squaring off with me in the center of a circle of cheering 9-year-olds. Naturally, I was hissing.

Yes. Hissing, sigh. The best thing to do when mocked is to revert to the subject of their mockery, right? I had found such power in pussydom that perhaps I hoped that I could pounce and claw my way to victory. This did not win me any fans and I was soon surrounded by chants pleading for Lindsay's victory. Indeed, she smacked me down quickly to the linoleum and I was left alone, crying, waiting with Lee's mom for mine to come pick me up.

It wasn't the last of my birthday debacles. I was always getting hurt at those things. The roller-skating rink was my den of torture. If I didn't fall on my knee or have my ankle run over, I would be strangled by a neon necklace. I knew things looked bad, I knew people were saying I was a baby. I tried to be careful. The last party I was invited to at the rink, I made it through the whole thing...until I crawled under the table to get my shoes and the damn thing collapsed on my head. Clearly, I was jinxed and therefore not much fun to have around. Funny how my parties always went off without a hitch.

Oh, I had good parties. My mom poured her every energy into the party I had that year, my birthday's proximity to Halloween making it a holiday bash. My best friend Sue and I were dueling Madonnas, along with more than half of the women in America that year. The fireplace was roaring with a dummy devil set up in the easy chair in front of it. It was just a mask and a cape on a large stuffed animal, but it never failed to scare me into screaming. The kids traveled down a cobweb-strewn stairway to my basement, which, as I've mentioned, was already frightening in itself. The boyfriend I'd settled on, Joey Kessler's friend Alex Pinsky, was there and he was a mummy. There was a piñata and also that Halloween game where you pass around peeled grapes in the dark and say they're eyeballs.

Things were good. Sue and me and Dana - of the 1st grade vomiting Dana - were a rotating repertory of best friends. We listened to Michael Jackson without discomfort and Milli Vanilli without irony. Alex, even though he wasn't bright, wouldn't kiss me and gave me lame pink stuffed animals as gifts, was my boyfriend and my teachers seemed to think that I was pretty neat.

Plus, there was that gifted program and this year, fifth grade, they were going to do the Scottish play. Macbeth. I suppose I can say it because I'm not in a theater right now. You can probably guess whom I wanted to play. Lady Macbeth? Heck no! Why stop there? Why be bound by gender propriety?

I'd already mastered interspecies roles, how much harder could playing a man be? I'd been taking children's acting courses on the weekends at the local university; I knew nobody else could do it. Certainly not Aaron Lubble whose stage presence was marred by a physicality that my mother likened to a pee-pee dance. So, I auditioned against all the boys and, with the aid of spirit gum, was soon a prepubescent, cross-gender Shakespearean anti-hero. At least for the first act. The play was trisected and presented by 3 gifted groups from other schools. Apparently, there were other schools! Who knew?

Given our tender age, we had permission to change tough passages - CHANGE THEM - but I relished the verse. Furthermore, I was appalled when in the 3rd act, Macbeth, now king, uttered upon hearing of his wife's demise, not the magnificent "Tomorrow and tomorrow" soliloquy, but simply "Oh my God." I knew enough to realize that this was the greatest tragedy of the evening. Tied for second was hearing the bard squawked in Long Island accents and pulling the fake beard hair off my chinny chin chin.

A woman from the crowd asked if I'd had speech lessons, I'd done so well. That's the difference. Were I a more privileged youth, in a more charming suburb, that woman could have been a big-city casting director. That's all it would've taken. That's how it happens for some, though admittedly, a mature viewing of the videotape proves my performance awful, with my mother and sister tittering all the way through. I don't know where my dad was. But my mom, so proud afterwards, presented me with a beautifully bound volume of Shakespeare's tragedies. I never opened it. Seems my fascination with the canon was only fleeting.

I tried to parlay my theatrical coup into a career. Still obsessed, I wrote a letter to "Cats" begging them to allow a kitten. They did write back saying I was too young and to stick with the track I was on until I could later audition. Sadly, sticking to the track I was on has proven too difficult.

SEVEN

I didn't even go to dancing school for much longer. I went to the same place as Abby, with whom I'd had the on-stage Catfight. We'd forgotten our differences, as kids can, and were intermittently close friends. Abby lived farther away than Sue and Dana, so it was harder. We used to take embarrassing pseudo-modeling pictures and say we had a band that we named "Silent Shadows." We had a couple of terrible songs, including an incredibly-dark-for-elementary-school title track. *Silent shadows, lonely shadows, they surround you, all around you.* Yikes. Mostly, we covered Madonna and Cyndi Lauper.

Abby was a good dancer and recommended this place to me, L'Ecole School of Classical Ballet. It was a serious, if redundantly named studio run by a tough Spaniard, Yasmin, and her idiot daughter, Reba. I was there three nights a week. I took jazz and ballet but had to drop out of tap. It flustered me. I couldn't remember the order of the steps and anxiety seized me, like it did with multiplication. Still, my proficiency in the other realms of dance was enough that I was asked to be in the company that toured competitively. I was so thrilled, sure it was a quick step to Cats from something like that.

My mom had to work late the first day that I had company rehearsal. I was nervous as I called Yasmin to tell her that I'd be late. She screamed at me, screamed. She said I had to get there however I could.

Now, my mom was none too pleased that this woman had said such a thing to her very-impressionable young daughter. Even though I hadn't, mom told Yasmin that I could've tried to walk or hitchhike, been kidnapped. Anything could have happened and it would've been her fault, my mother said. She also said I'd never be going back to that school.

We'd already paid for my two recital costumes, but in an effort to smooth things over, mom didn't demand her money back. She said we'd take the costumes. The jazz costume was black leggings and an oversized shirt, always welcome in the wardrobe of the times. The ballet costume was a magnificent cobalt confection, usable in the very least for Halloween. If I'd ever gotten that dress, I might've come home from school and put it on every day, just to feel good.

But I never did get that dress. When we heard from Abby that the costumes had come in, we gave a call over to Yasmin. Dimwitted Reba answered and said we could come and pick them up. When we picked up the bag and brought it home, we didn't find the costumes, no. In their stead was a pair of tights and a large shirt they sold at the in-house dance shop. My princess pixie prom dress was reduced to a white crinoline - just a crinoline, mind you - no skirts or undergarments. This arrest-inducing ensemble was completed by a Pepto-Bismol pink petticoat, its arms six inches longer than my own, its allotment for breasts far more than I required, and its neckline plunging all the way to my navel, where a single button held it all together. My mom was livid.

We called the studio and recorded the conversation, gleeful in our righteousness. Reba said Yasmin was away. "Where," we asked. Reba stammered, "She's on an island." Long Island, mom and I joked. Mom threatened court. She told Reba that my heart was broken.

We wound up getting half the money back. An imposing male neighbor – Larry and Robert's dad - went with us to get it. He had a look that hovered between lawyer and mobster. I don't know why my own dad didn't go with us, and I don't know why we didn't get all the money. We were certainly entitled to all of it. I don't know why my mom settled for less. Just in general.

EIGHT

I still had acting classes, at least. Had my mother been willing to be of the stage variety, who knows what would have happened? The woman who ran my acting school approached her once. Eady said I really had something and that she wanted to manage me, she would take me around to auditions and everything. Here I was 45 minutes out of the city, everything I wanted so close and now being offered to me. Mom was scared though. Scared of what, I'm not sure. The business, my sensitivity, the world. I can't say that I would have been successful, necessarily, or that things would have turned out well if I had been. I could have wound up a real monster, another child star casualty. Everything for a reason, right? Right.

So, no dancing, and no acting…what COULD I turn my starved attentions to? By the time I was 10 and my sister 16, she had had a succession of suitors who intrigued me with their virile and fully-formed young man-ness. I would haunt Carrie and her dates and spent much of my time being shooed away. Carrie and I got along much better now though. She told me that hanging out with me was like hanging out with people her own age, the prospect of which thrilled me. People are always telling me I seem much older than my years, that I am an "old soul." I doubt that. I feel like the experience of life is brand new to me, and I am horrified by it. I do have a tendency toward using antiquated old-world phrases, but I think that's more because I read a lot, rather than having been reincarnated. If it is the latter, I don't think I'm getting it right this time either. This desk I'm sitting at doesn't seem to think so. Unless sluts are exalted in the afterlife.

But anyway, Carrie even went so far as to let me drop in on a party she had in our basement. Perhaps that was my mother's work, though, thinking my presence a policing one. It didn't work though. Few high school parties occur without alcohol and I was terribly confused by the drunken young folk, particularly the vomiting guy. I wondered why anyone would go to a party while so sick.

I think I actually hoped to be picked up by some handsome junior. I was definitely flirting and overly pleased by the use of the word cute. Thankfully, my sister had no Humbert-y peers and I was eventually shepherded away, disappointed. So instinctively was I drawn to the prospect of snaring and pleasing the male species that I can't remember a time when it wasn't my primary focus.

Apparently, it ran in the family. On a sleepy Sunday afternoon at my grandmother's house, Carrie and I were curled on the sofa and she told me in hushed tones about sex, and giving a blowjob to a guy in our basement. I said "ew," but I was mesmerized. I'm not sure how liberal my sister was with the dispensation of oral sex, but I do know that once I walked with my mother to our local strip mall to stamp out an epithet directed at my sister. Carrie had written her name in the fresh poured concrete only to have someone etch 'is a slut' beneath it. Whether it was true or just some misogynist-in-training extolling a hypothesis he would've written under any woman's name, we can't be sure. "Someone said something mean about Carrie," mom explained, assuming I didn't understand. To me though it was tantamount to fame, like having your name in front of Graumann's Chinese. And the word slut, it sounded filthy and alluring, mysterious and powerful. Perhaps in the recesses of my mind, I decided that day that I would be a slut too, and news of my triumphs could spread across desktops everywhere.

NINE

Being a slut was going to be tough considering boys in my school didn't much like me. When I started junior high, we'd been placed in a larger pool with kids from another elementary school in Levittown. Now, I don't know if you know about Levittown. It's kind of famous for being crappy. It's the first "planned community," or something, tract houses built for men coming home from World War 2. In "Little Shop of Horrors," Audrey says she wants a little house off the interstate, not somewhere fancy like Levittown. That's a joke.

My erstwhile boyfriend Alex Pinsky was in another group of classes, so we broke up by default. Sue and Dana were in another group too. I didn't know anyone that first day I walked into sixth grade. When we all introduced ourselves, I said that I was an actress and somebody chortled. It was probably Brian. Brian von Essen came up to me before class began and asked if I was Jewish. When I said that I wasn't, he snorted and said, "You're kidding." I'd never experienced that kind of hate. Most of the kids in the area where I'd grown up were Jewish. I didn't really make anything of it, they were my friends. I wrote in my diary that night wondering if Brian was "some sort of religious bigot."

Our school was now divided by SRK's and LDB's, Seaford Rich Kids and Levittown Dirt Bags. I wasn't rich, I knew that much. My parents had a baby blue Datsun and that old brown station wagon. Still, I admit that I was spoiled. Boy, was I turned out that first day of class. My sister worked at Pants Plus, a sort of bad 80's fashion Shangri-La. Her friend Lena was my size, and "procured" for me a far-too-mature long black pencil-slim skirt, with a white Surf Fetish "Surfers in the City" t-shirt. On it were men in business suits with surfboards. If it were any more 80's an outfit, it would've come with its own beating synthesizer. She accessorized me with a black leather belt to sling low on my waist and loop in the front. It was easily a $150 outfit. She said she'd used her discount, but I'm pretty sure this particular discount was of the five-finger ilk. That was cool. My sister stole too. She'd taken a Precious Moments from a local card store and given it to our mother for Christmas. Those things are in glass cases too, so for our age that was some crazy "Ocean's Eleven" shit. I'd just managed some lipsticks to this point.

That Christmas I got a rabbit. I guess my parents (wrongly) figured I'd done so well with the smaller animals, they might as well try me on something larger. I considered a name from "Watership Down," but settled on Addison, big fan as I was of the show "Moonlighting." Addison was beige with grey ears, feet and tail. He was very possibly the cutest thing ever. He got loose in the backyard one time, or maybe I let him go to see what would happen. That could've been his ticket to freedom right there, but he didn't take it, no. He hopped right on back to my arms. He passed the test. He loved me.

Carrie's friend Lena died in a car accident later that year. It was right outside the high school parking lot. As our bus pulled up that day, her little brother looked out the window excitedly exclaiming, "Oh shit, there's a huge accident. I bet somebody died!" And I'd bet you anything he felt really bad about saying that when he was called to the office that day and they told him it was his sister who was dead.

Mom wouldn't let me go pay my respects, thinking a young person's funeral too upsetting to be my first. So that day, instead, I went to school in the outfit that she had given me. My lunch mates and I were sparring coquettishly with the table of boys next to us. While futzing with a soda can, one of the guys cut his hand and he splashed the blood from his resultant wound onto my white shirt, marring the surfers in their city.

The juxtaposition of blood on the dead girl's gift freaked me out and I went hysterical. Probably made him feel pretty badly about what he'd done. I had a tendency to be slightly dramatic, but then, life seemed to have that tendency too.

Addison didn't last the year either. He'd spent the first winter caged in the basement, where his smell overpowered. By spring we'd moved him to a beautiful two room hutch underneath the birch tree in the backyard. I don't know if he could have withstood the winter cold out there. I thought rabbits were outside all the time. It didn't matter. I didn't give him a chance to survive it, forgetting as I did to feed him.

My mom reminded me one night. The shock and guilt washed over me. "It hasn't been that long," I stammered, "I'll go now." My father went with me. He probably knew. We trudged through the snow and lifted the wooden hutch door. "No, see, he's fine," I said, seeing him curled in the corner of the hutch. My dad poked Addison with a stick and his light, stiff body lifted. I screamed. I was such a little asshole. Such a stupid little asshole. To this day, it may be the thing I feel most guilty about in my life. And that's saying A LOT.

TEN

My family took a vacation together to Colonial Williamsburg. Everyone was tense the whole time. Carrie was away from her boyfriend, my parents hated each other and I... I was just there. We all stayed in a shitty motel room together. I crawled into bed with my mom and dad one morning to see a cockroach entering the place that I had vacated. I'd never seen one before. This was certainly an educational excursion. We visited the old-fashioned town to see metal smiths and candle-dippers. It bored the holy living hell out of my sister and me. We needed some excitement, so we made it a thieving vacation. The sprawling gift shoppe and its anachronistic selection of goods became our prey. I eyed a porcelain figurine of a mouse wearing a tutu, a pearly pink nail polish, a mood ring, a horoscope scroll. My sister filled a bag as well. We were girls gone wild. We went into the stained and broken motel bathroom to compare our booty.

I stole for the rush, for the forbidden aspect. I certainly didn't need anything. Not that I got everything I wanted, but I didn't lack for anything. Not anything tangible. I was spoiled, yeah. I ate Fluffernutters with Sundances for lunch every day. They were these sparkling fruity beverages that looked like wine coolers, and used Van Morrison's "Moondance" for their ads. I liked the song, I liked the drink. No box drinks for me, my palate was oh-so-refined. You know, unless you count the peanut butter and marshmallow sandwiches. I couldn't eat cafeteria food. Never could.

ELEVEN

I ran for 6th grade president and lost to a nerdy young man. Smart guy, not undeserving, I don't begrudge him his victory. I joined the communications club and got to read the morning announcements over the loudspeaker. It afforded me that sweet, sweet attention that I thrived on.

No guys liked me. Guys didn't seem to like anyone yet, except for Tina and Corinne, two prematurely robust young ladies. Despite all efforts, I did not have my first kiss until the summer following.

My first kiss was, predictably, at summer camp. Driftwood, the same one in which I'd made my failed foray into child pornography three years prior. I was getting more attention from the boys at camp. Small wonder, as they had spent far less time with me. This overly spiked-haired boy, Andy, was my theoretical boyfriend for three days during which I'm not sure we spoke at all. But then there was Ryan. He was a junior counselor and a couple of years older. After a week of "dating," or sharing popsicles on the way to the buses, he took me into the trees and planted one on me. It was the last day of camp. We walked into the clearing where I saw his friend walking towards us with his own nubile camper, mouthing, "Did you?" Ryan nodded to the affirmative and was met with a high five. Ahhh, innocence, where men are given kudos for kisses. Ryan would call in the coming weeks saying that it sucked that we couldn't see each other. It didn't so much bother me. I suddenly found him annoying and clingy. He'd served his purpose. I was done with him.

I was ready to bring my newfound experience back to school. I painted my nails a pearly pink and tried on my new back-to-school Benetton outfit for my mom. I held up my hand for her to check out my manicure job. "Where'd you get that color?", she immediately asked. "It was in the cabinet," I retorted quickly. She made me go get it and my heart pounded as I returned to her. "I saw you with that in Williamsburg," she leveled at me, "did you steal it?" "No," I cried, so utterly caught, "I bought it." I swore. I wept. "I can't believe you think I'd do that!" I wailed. She seemed so cold to me, in her anger and disappointment. I collapsed at her side, longing for her to hug me, so that I knew that she still loved me. I cried in her reluctant arms. "Jaime," she said curiously, "raise your arm for me." I said, "What?", but I did it. She sniffed deeply. "Jaime, I think you smell!" "No!" I said. She told me it was okay, that it was natural. I was so embarrassed, but she seemed sort of proud. I was becoming a woman.

TWELVE

I started 7th grade confident. I wore deodorant and a bra, however useless the latter was. I had a crush on Mike Crespi, who looked kinda like Corey Feldman at a time when that was a good thing. Sue and Dana were back in my lunch period so we all got to sit together again. We sat with Tina, Corinne and some other new Levittown girls. They were all pretty girls. Some of them were cheerleaders. There weren't school cheerleaders yet; Levittown had a local football league with their own. They were the Red Devils, their uniforms in fierce red and black. Their league had already formed, much to my chagrin, as I would've liked to join them. They didn't seem very inclusive.

I ran for 7th grade president. I was surprised that, when I was introduced to give my speech, I got all this enthusiastic applause. I was visibly taken aback and the crowd laughed. I won.

For a junior high administration, my regime was a powerful one. I used my office to enact change for the betterment of the class. Well, okay…I did set up a destined-to-be-ignored suggestion box and hold contests, which is more than is accomplished by most school officers, whom I am convinced are largely figureheads.

In the first contest you had to guess how many holiday M&M's were in a giant fishbowl and the 1st, 2nd and 3rd place winners got stuffed stockings of appropriately diminishing size. The next one was a drawing, and three people won beach packages, with coolers, towels, sun block and the like. It was pretty great, or rather, it would've been pretty great had the Red Devil Vice President and I not rigged it so that our friends won. We folded their names extra tight, and laid them in the corners of the drawing box. Desperate to gain his affection, I chose Mike Crespi and my veep chose her cheerleader friend. Absolute power corrupts, absolutely...and I suppose piffling power poisons perilously.

We were not concertedly evil, however. The third drawing we left to chance, resulting in the win of a girl I'd truly never heard of. It was a good balance, I thought, sure to throw off suspicion. I was kidding myself though. This was junior high...there were no such things as secrets.

THIRTEEN

In a move befitting my growing ambitions, I dabbled in film and gaming. Kinda. Sue and I were inspired to make a treasure hunt sort-of-thing for Dana. There were pieces of puzzles for her to find, each with the clue to the next one on the other side, and the entirety of which, itself, would be a clue. It was pretty complex, but the eventual treasure was a single piece of garlic gum. When Dana came across the elements of the game prior to its execution, we improbably dismissed it as relating to a movie my sister had recorded off the television while up at college in Connecticut. The movie was called "Teraskull," as was the game.

Clearly now, a film needed to be made to back up our falsehood. We would make this movie and we would say that it was the one my sister taped. God bless youth and its ability to oversee the logical gaps that rendered ridiculous such an undertaking. Sue and I would show it to Dana before she played the game.

Teraskull is a pirate. He becomes such when spurned by the townswoman he loves, who thinks him sleazy. He murders her. He then falls in love once more whilst out on the high seas, between various bouts of pillaging. This includes an incident called the Stockholm Massacre in which paper people on sticks made of straws "run" madly through a 4-panel cartoon diorama, being thrown up in the air as they are killed to a soundtrack of mouth-rockets.

Though she admits being turned on by his violent nature, Teraskull's pirate babe sadly thinks him a sleaze as well, and he thusly kills her and swears off women. Really. He "becomes homosexual" and takes up with Roy G. Biv, a fellow pirate who eventually joins the Mormons (sure, why not?), calls Teraskull sleazy and gets the rainbow named after him. Pretty heady, progressive stuff for 7th grade. It's a half hour long, single static camera affair, complete with commercials and a basement-piano soundtrack. Rather than memorizing all the lines, we prerecorded them and moved our lips vaguely to match the words as they played.

The close of the film brings us to present time, where two boys, Brandon and Mikey - or Sue and I in drag assuming the names of the boys we had crushes on - discover Teraskull's treasure map. You know, just sitting around in one of their basements. In another pictorial representation, they find tunnels under the house. Searching through the darkness, they are confronted by the ghosts of Teraskull, trying to retain his treasure from beyond the grave, and Roy G. Biv, who turns out to be Mikey's great-great-great grandfather. Roy convinces Mikey not to take the treasure so that future generations may enjoy searching for it. Mikey concedes that "ancestry is more important than riches" and leaves the treasure be, much to Brandon's consternation. "When you're a bum drinking 89 cent liquor, don't come crying to me," he says as my father pressed the fade-out button. It was very popular up at UCONN, where it made the rounds of my sisters' group of theater friends. Teraskull even would have made the UCONN paper 10-best list if it hadn't been deemed too much of an inside joke. It is just that sort of politicking that has repressed me all my life, I imagine.

Once the film screened for Dana, she was presented with the game, the idea being that she was now to search for Teraskull's treasure, the garlic gum. Resistant to figuring out the clues set before her, we led her around the house, answering the questions, and putting the puzzle together.

I didn't realize that I might be alienating either of my friends by doing this. It seems to me an awfully fun thing to do, though I'm sure I was fairly totalitarian in the running of it. I do recall making an effort to include the commercials Sue had written, despite their complete and utter inferiority to my own. I didn't ever point out that mine were better, of course. I'd learned my lesson about that in kindergarten.

FOURTEEN

Still, I guess I did something, had been doing something. I know this because one night I got a call. It was Rena Schneider. She was one of Sue and Dana's friends from the other side of town. She said she didn't like what I was doing to them. I still don't know what that was. She said I wasn't to sit at their lunch table anymore.

The next day at school, I walked around in a terrified shock. Tina saw me before lunch and asked if I was going. I told her about the call as tears filled my eyes. She said she knew about it, but thought it was mean. Of course, I could still eat lunch with them.

It was strained. I offered that if any of them wanted anything from the lunch line, I could buy it. Someone audibly groaned. I acknowledge that it was a pretty weak move. I could feel the disdain swirl around me.

I didn't even try to sit there the next day, or ever again. I became transient, sipping my Sundance with whoever would have me, or sometimes alone. I still went to birthday parties for a while, likely due to parentally-enforced reciprocation. At Corinne's, I did a backbend and landed on my head. At Tina's pool party, the girls mockingly asked about my former relationship with Alex Pinsky. I said that I knew it was over at our grade-school graduation. See, I had requested that the DJ play what I deemed our song, "Stand by Me," and it turned out to be warped.

"Warped?" they all said and laughed. They laughed, not at my joke, but that I'd said it. I realize now they didn't really understand the word, but at the time, I felt like the idiot. We all jumped in the pool. "Look out, Jaime," Sharon said, "I'm going to warp you." Everybody laughed. They were laughing at me, at how fucking stupid I was. In the crowd I felt alone, and scared. Sharon was a tough girl, maybe she would warp me.

When I made new friends, they were girls from the other school, a few LDBs. We didn't talk the same way or like the same things, but they were there. I went to a sleepover at Lorilee's house. When they were in high school together, Lorilee's older sister had fought with mine over a guy. The whole family was pretty widely acknowledged to be trash, according to Carrie, anyway. To walk into her house was to know why. It was small, dark, dirty. It was sad. Her bedroom's ceiling shared the 45-degree angle of the roof. We played some kind of truth or dare game and then came the Ouija board.

Something weird happened, honestly. Surely there is no group more given to hysteria than prepubescent girls, but this was for real. We were talking to a young girl who had been killed. It didn't feel manipulated. Someone started crying and said we should stop. The pointer jumped off the board. We were all shaken. We went to sleep.

The pain woke me up. It was behind my eyes and stabbing. The daggers prodded through to the center of my brain. I writhed, I screamed, I puked. I learned that Kara, another guest at the party who had leukemia, had gotten sick during the night too, and had already gone home. It was 4 am and mom was coming to get me. The next morning, they found Lorilee's back window broken. I kept having those headaches.

I called them screamers. The screaming and the crying didn't help, of course, but only increased the unbearable pressure in my head. Eventually I would just exhaust myself into unconsciousness. On came the doctors. When my head hurt so much one night that my mother took me to the hospital for sedation, it began a succession of neurologists and ear, nose and throat men. I had clogged sinuses and they considered surgery to drain them. We found a specialist and I went to the hospital for a week. While there, it came about that my sinuses weren't really clogged enough that surgery was necessary. Maybe there were other factors involved? Maybe stress?

Noooo, couldn't be. I continued on in my enrichment classes, at the top of the high honor roll. I was always being told that I was not working to potential. That was ridiculous. How much better was I supposed to do? It doesn't get any higher than high honor roll. I was doing just fine...though I had something approaching an allergic reaction to homework.

It was funny that I was the President. My position became ammunition in the onslaught of taunts I withstood. The best friends I'd ever had were gone. Worse than gone, they would join in the snickers as I was concertedly mocked by the class. I was terrified to have to give a presentation in front of my health class of "things that are special to me." I knew I'd be judged for whatever I brought. Nothing that I could choose would be beyond reproach. I didn't know what to pick. My head roiled and broiled over my few options. Nothing was special to me. People tittered as I showed my wares. I felt myself shrinking.

"That's all I have," I said, "my life hasn't been very consequential." They all laughed. At me. "No, no, that was very nice," said Mr. Goodman, the health teacher that everyone liked. His very name was a beacon of hope to me. He made sympathetic eye contact. That was the most I ever got.

My jacket was stolen from my locker. Nobody locked their lockers in school, see, but it looked like I would have to start. Even my enrichment classes weren't an escape anymore. Most of my tormentors were smart kids too, which just meant that they had the capacity to better craft their attacks. Aaron Lubble was still in there, for one, and a new foe in the form of cute but compact Lance Nardo. My project to make a Greek myth-related tourism ad resulted in lambastes from the group as I called myself "Elvira" to tout the pleasures of visiting

Hades. "You wish you were Elvira," Aaron and Lance chortled, referring to the buxom Halloween icon. I wasn't trying to be her at all; I just thought it was an evil name. You know, for selling Hades.

It really was a pretty clever ad, not that anything could be heard above the jeers. No, I was not safe, even amongst the other nerds. To be sure, Robbie Ringero, who had once had a crush on me, sent message by way of a classmate that I was a pirate's dream. I smiled with appreciation - someone did still like me! - until the fellow finished that I was such because of my sunken chest. I don't know what was expected of my body, but clearly I wasn't meeting the standard set by my milk-fed peers. A song was created to herald my bustlessness, to the tune of the old doo-wop ditty "Chain Gang." In my version, the lyrics were altered to say, "That's the sound of the men working on Jai-meee." The sound referred to was that of the singer rubbing his hand against any available flat surface. I suppose I had to give them points for creativity.

I know it's probably pretty standard middle-school torture. Maybe I was even lucky in comparison to others, but I wasn't prepared. I didn't understand. Nobody told me that everything would be okay.

I'd come home to an empty house and cry after a long bus ride of two-for-flinching where I got punched in the arm twice, even if I hadn't flinched. As I sat in the den before the television, writhing in existential angst and hormonal overload, I asked God for help. Make this pain go away, I begged aloud. Lift this tremendous pressure from off my head. I felt nothing in response.

FIFTEEN

My sister visited from college. She brought with her a new boyfriend, a liberal viewpoint and a Depeche Mode tape. She played it for me. This was phenomenal. God DOES have a sick sense of humor, just like they say! I started writing Depeche Mode on my notebooks next to Poison, Def Leppard and Guns n' Roses, which was the order of the day. But I wasn't long for the top 40 world. Carrie also tuned me in to WDRE, Long Island's alternative radio station. As the announcer introduced a new track from Siouxsie and the Banshees, I snorted that if I had a band, I wouldn't name them after a bunch of screaming she-devils. But then they played the song "Peek-a-Boo," and it was awesome. It even had a twisted variation of the refrain my mother used to sing to me. Except that, whereas my mom would question the origin of my peepers, Siouxsie wondered about my weepers, which was certainly more appropriate for me of late. It was the same, but darker. Right up my alley.

Carrie asked me about my kindergarten boyfriend, good ol' Lyle Caruthers. I informed her that he was a fag now, not in the gay way, but in the 1980's adolescent sense that meant 'lame.' She and her boyfriend Graham looked at each other in dismay. "We don't say that," she said, "that's not nice." I never said it again.

Carrie had moved from an attempt at sorority life into the theater department. She stage-managed plays and hung out with neat people that made improvised movies on video. I longed for that life. Mom and I went up to see one of the shows and during a tour of the theater I vaingloriously commandeered the stage to recapture my triumph with one of Macbeth's soliloquies. This nearly caused department-wide coronaries, it being opening night, and Macbeth being the widely acknowledged theatrical curse. Oops. I was led outside to perform the turning and spitting ritual that would cleanse the theater of my crime.

Carrie told me she knew that I was having a tough time. She told me that people from our school were assholes, and to ignore them. All our past rivalry seemed vanquished. She told me that I was a neat kid, and that everything was going to be okay.

But she was never there.

Nobody ever seemed to be there. I had three hours to kill before anyone else got home. I killed them dancing in the basement. I killed them shouting angry songs I made up while crying. I killed them screaming out the kitchen window like a monster as kids from the elementary school walked home past our house, laughing hysterically as they stopped still and looked around in terror for the source.

I would hang out once in a while with these girls Lara and Farrah, also from "the other side of town." I could tell Farrah didn't like me. I didn't blame her. Nobody else did either. Once, Lara's older sister got us wine coolers. Aside from the holiday nips of amaretto that I was allowed by my parents, given to me – in retrospect – to calm my ass down, it was my first time drinking. We ordered pizza and watched the Rocky Horror Picture Show. Knowing it was a bastion of counterculture, I expected to love it, but was very disappointed.

So, what were we to do, young girls besot with liquor and boredom? We asked over some boys, including my crush, Mike Crespi. They suggested strip poker. I was the only girl stupid and desperate enough to join them. As I sat there losing, I tried to crush together what little additional flesh had risen on my chest, to create the illusion of substance. Lara acknowledged my action under her breath from the sofa, "Squeeeeze." Farrah sat next to her, disgusted. I stared, intrigued, at the uncontrolled bulge in Mike's pants. I sidled closer to him. I made it pretty clear that I was available for the taking. There were no takers.

SIXTEEN

The soundtrack of the time infused my confused mind with lust and need. Top forty radio was an onslaught of sex-starved singers. Like a virgin. I want your sex. Naughty girls need love too. The latter was sung by a former porn star who seemed the very height of alluring danger and made the boys drool. All these songs by bleating women over synthesized beats, they spelled out the way. They wrote my position. The song "Easy Lover" was the soundtrack to my nighttime fantasies. As I lay in bed attempting sleep, I imagined myself the titular lover. I, too, would steal men's hearts and leave them begging. In my mind I walked on the beach at night, bonfires lighting my way as I seduced men in my oceanfront tent.

My mom finally told me about sex, and I had to pretend that my sister hadn't already done so. Well, mom didn't so much tell me about sex as she played a movie about it. So clinical, no context. The only statement she offered on the topic was that she and I were "very sexual people, and had to be careful." I'm still not sure what that meant.

Lara, Farrah and I went to a local guido party. I assure you that guidos are a self-proclaimed and proud social subset on Long Island, and I am therefore not being culturally insensitive. Rob Barone (who pronounced the "e" at the end of his name to up the Italian factor) asked me upstairs. We kissed and groped to "Bust a Move" and Tone-Loc's "Wild Thing." Don't just stand there, bust a move, she loves to do the wild thing. Downstairs, the other guys and my friends laughed. I was told later that they were touching and licking the wall, emulating what was being done to my similarly surfaced body upstairs. Rob told me he wasn't a virgin, that he'd slept with this girl in Canada. I didn't know that guys actually used that Canada thing. He tried to teach me to give him a hand job. I'd never touched a penis before. I didn't do it for long because I didn't know what I was doing, and I hate to do anything that I am not good at.

We went back to Lara's and I gushed excitedly about the events amid the exchange of looks. As we all got into our sleeping bags, I put on this movie I'd brought, "Heathers." I'd heard about it and it sounded just great. Everyone else fell asleep as I sat transfixed as my twisted outsider fantasy played itself out before me. We even had three popular girls named Heather in my school. I imagined myself Winona Ryder, exacting my revenge on the popular regime with a Christian Slater bad boy by my side. If only some guy would have me. I knew it wasn't Rob. We had nothing in common; I didn't even really like him. It was just that he was showing me interest that made him attractive to me. Besides, Rob didn't even talk to me after that night.

I didn't hang out much with Lara and Farrah either, anymore. One of the last times, Lara brought some of her sister's cigarettes and we tried smoking in the church parking lot near my house. I had to lay down afterward, my head spinning. Some boys came by from the local Catholic school and I was drawn to one of them right away. He was drawn back, I could tell. Despite my previous misadventures, I recall this as my first moment of actual sexual tension. He smoked cigarettes and talked of being suspended. He was bad. He was sexy. He was Jack, Jack Abito. We had the same initials, and my burgeoning fatalist swooned. We made plans to meet there the next week, on the same day mom had gotten Lara and me tickets to see Midnight Oil. Lara didn't like them, or me anymore, but she wasn't averse to seeing a free show.

When Mom came back from work the day of the show, I was gone. I was down at the church playground, exchanging phone numbers, innuendoes and fevered glances with my intended paramour. When I got home, mom was the fevered one. She was furious. I'd not left a note, so she didn't know what had happened to me. She ripped up the concert tickets in front of my face. I wept at the unfairness of it all as mom drove Lara home. There would be no socially conscious Australian rock for us that evening.

I found solace in the fact that I had traded music for a chance at love. But Jack never called me. After waiting a suitably ladylike length of time, I called him, assuming that, considering our connection, he must have lost my number. The phone rang, and he answered. Jack pretended he was someone else, and said he wasn't there. I wasn't an idiot, I knew it was him on the other end, but I said okay and hung up. I didn't understand what was going on, but I knew two things. That I deserved an explanation and that I could pretend too. I called back an hour later. I inflated my voice, making it chirpy and bright. He answered again and admitted he had done so. I dropped my ruse and came clean. "Look, I'm sorry I did that, but I just want to know what happened."

"My friend thought you were ugly," he replied. Couldn't argue with that. I wished him a nice life and the ability to think for himself. That was that. I was despondent.

There was a box of crayons and markers in the drawer next to my bed. It was a craft box, gone long unused. There was an Exact-o knife in there too. I don't know why, or where it came from, but there it was. I traced small lines in my arms and dabbed up the blood with tissues. I drew in the soft flesh of my inner wrist, where I knew it would be covered by my watch. I etched lightly into the veins that stuck out most. I got ambitious and traveled up my arm, made the cuts deeper, made them x's to lie beneath my watch's band. I could look at my marks during the day in school and know that I had somewhere to go when the day was done.

SEVENTEEN

During a scrabble game with my visiting cousin, mom noticed the cuts and asked what they were. I blamed them, despite their inconsistent angles, on Lara's cat. Mom didn't say anything. She knew I hadn't been to Lara's in weeks.

Suddenly, I was back at the neurologist. It only proves the naivety of my mother and the times, that this seemed the appropriate specialist for me. I don't know why mom took me back to him, other than the fact that there was clearly something wrong in my head. Mom left the room. I stood opposite him, awkward, revealed. Everything in the room seemed so bright, it was swollen, it vibrated. The doctor confronted me about my wounds and I admitted to their origin. He asked why, and I said I didn't know. The reasons why are clear-cut now, of course, pardon the pun. A physical badge of emotional pain and blah blah blah, but I don't know where I got the idea. Cutting wasn't then what it is now. The media blitz and concurrent 'cutting clubs' were several years off. So, why did I do it? It came so naturally. It astounded me later on to hear there were others who did the same. It further astounded me to hear that 90% of cutters were sexually abused. I didn't remember anything like that ever happening to me, but for a while I thought I might be suppressing the memory.

I was thusly sent to my first of many therapists. She was clinical and cold. Lots of questions, but no answers. Do you think about hurting yourself? Do you think about killing yourself? Do you have a plan? How often do you have these feelings? How does that make you feel?

It didn't make me feel any less alienated, that's for sure. I squirmed under the microscope. I had started 8th grade, and decided to run for class president again. This time, though, overdeveloped Tina of the erstwhile lunch table was running against me. The therapist advised against my candidacy. It seemed odd to have someone that's supposed to help you try to thwart your ambitions. Perhaps she knew beforehand that Tina would be wearing a miniskirt when she gave her speech up on that stage.

I lost. Of course, I lost. How could I do anything but lose in the face of such competition? I ran with the promise of more fun contests, but I ignored the inherent corruption of my regime. I could easily ignore my own inequity. I had done a good job. Tina wouldn't. She would be a figurehead with boobs. A figureboob. Further, this was president of the whole junior high, and the entire student body got to vote. Tina had a little brother - ridiculously named Tino - in 6th grade. I knew what I was getting into. I truly believed that I deserved to win. I had set myself up for the fall. I could have run for another office unopposed. There wasn't much in the way of spirit in our school.

Sitting next to Tina when the results of the election came in, I congratulated her out of the side of my mouth before her name was even called.

I spent that year without a lunch table to call home, hanging out with whoever asked, usually not more than once. I even went to the house of an awkward girl I had mocked in gym class two years prior. Carissa made me draw her a shoe and autograph it. She said it was amazing and hung it over her bed. She said she couldn't believe I was hanging out with her. Who the fuck was I?

EIGHTEEN

Despite the lack of friends, boyfriends, and the general widespread derision of myself, I found it of utmost importance to attend the quarterly school dances. I went to all of them and managed to cry at every one. Not about the dancing, usually about a boy. I always had such high expectations, such grandiloquent romances played out in my head that came nowhere near fruition in reality. No boy would even dance with me. I thought I was a pretty good dancer, but nobody ever told me so. Sometimes when people are good at things, other people tell them so. It's a far more pleasant thing to do than pointing out their flaws.

That's one of my theories on why attractive women tend to have low self-esteem. When you have a homely chick, people are always saying, "Oh, she has nice hair," or "she has pretty eyes." But a beautiful woman is dissected differently. They'll point out her chubby thighs or big nose. For example.

My father's nose is huge, my mother's is tiny and mine falls somewhere on the spectrum closer to dad's. Mom used to tell me she'd fear whilst I was in her womb that I'd arrive with her small eyes and dad's large proboscis, rendering me a hideous mole-child. Fortunately, as my uncle once said, I had mom's pupils with dad's sockets: large, deep brown peepers that used to make my mom sing golly jeepers. She said they were like a shark's eyes. Dark, empty holes.

My nose was not excessively large, but was probably why people were always guessing I was Jewish. Embarrassingly, a summer camp swim coach asked if I was Jewish and I replied by asking him if he was asking me that because my nose was big. He said no, he was asking because his name was Jaime too, and that he was Jewish. He asked why I'd asked him what I had about my nose. Knowing I'd been busted in the propagation of a stereotype, I coolly answered that my query had been unrelated. I had asked him if my nose was big because I'd just banged it on the side of the pool. So smooth. Like a pane of glass...so transparent and smooth.

It was the year of the Mitzvahs, and since I had to go to some of my peers' parties, my mother, in a likely effort to cheer me, threw a huge coming-of-age birthday party for me, gentile-style. I still feel the anxiety of that day. I took the day off school, and mom didn't go to work. We tried to find an outfit for me. Nothing looked right. I got my haircut and that wasn't right either. Nothing was right. I'd invited all the usual suspects, even though they wouldn't normally so much as eat with me. We had a DJ that played some Depeche Mode by request, but mainly stayed to the hip-hop and hard rock course of the day.

There was a game of Spin the Bottle, with a prize given to the longest kiss. Mark Lanzer and I were the first to use open mouth, but several couples soundly thwarted our efforts thereafter. Mark was beautiful, and after his attentions of that evening, I became wholly obsessed with him. He told me he liked my haircut - he noticed! We slow-danced to Cher. "If I Could Turn Back Time." At the end of the night, though, I corralled Rob Barone for a non-contest kiss, and one that would outlast the night's winner. I wanted to have had the longest kiss. It was my birthday. It was a good party.

My dad caught me cursing. Most of the young revelers had left and I was opening my presents amongst a small throng. Back at the center of attention, I could always be counted on to go too far to maintain that position. "Holy shit, Robbie Ringero gave me 25 fucking dollars!" I exclaimed, charming little lady that I was. Dad threw me a look and I laughed. I could be pretty tough sometimes.

NINETEEN

I was in a new acting class at a local theater and I got drafted from there to do their children's shows. We were even getting paid a whopping $5 a show and sometimes our pictures would be in the paper. It started with "Cinderella," and I was one of the ugly stepsisters. Ahem. We preferred "wicked" stepsisters. We wore musty old costumes with pit stains of children past and performed for kids half our age. It was a lot of fun, a safe creative haven.

I tried to keep myself busy, but no occupation was great enough to quiet my mind. I liked working, liked money. In addition to my theatrical pittance, I had a paper route that brought a steady flow of cash. Truly, that is a torturous job not worth its efforts. I must have been a tragicomic sight to behold: a rather small girl toting 50 pounds of papers on a bike through all kinds of weather, and attempting to extract payment from neighbors like teeth from the mouthless. Few positions garner the disrespect of a paper-delivery child. The time you collect is invariably inopportune, and often you receive a slice of the home's angst with your tip. I did make several babysitting connections along my route, thus garnering me a fairly cushy income for a 13-year-old.

I had so much that I wanted to give back. Sally Struthers alerted me to the struggles of children in Africa. For only $.32 a day or something, I could sponsor one of these sad kids that looked imploringly at the camera in these ubiquitous commercials. I would be sent a picture! They would be a pen-pal! I imagined the satisfaction of forming this sort of benevolent friendship. Mom was supportive and proud of my gesture.

But then they sent me her picture. There were no flies in her eyes, no painfully protruding bones. A girl no younger than me, she looked smilingly at the camera. Her boobs were bigger than mine. I decided she was doing fine. Thus, ended my attempt at philanthropy.

Instead, I surrounded myself with all the luxuries a child can imagine: a television, a VCR and a new bike. I delivered papers for about a year, my will to do so depleting steadily all the while. By the end my mom would have to sharply remind me of my duty. I would beg her, sometimes crying, to drive me on my route. She never would, and she was right not to. A paper route teaches responsibility. I would believe that if I hadn't turned out so damn irresponsible.

I was ensconced by unnamed distress, overwhelming pressure, ephemeral anxiety. Even the theater was barely keeping me afloat. I was lucky I kept getting cast in the shows, because each time I did one, I told myself that when the run ended, I would kill myself. But, when one run ended, the rehearsals for the next had already begun.

After Cinderella was "Peter & the Wolf," in which I was the cat. Of course, this was tremendously satisfying to me. The shows were all audience participation plays, so kids from the awkward to the brash trod upon the stage with us, charged with menial tasks like helping "Cinderella clean up" or doing whatever Peter did with that wolf. I finally got the lead in "Rumplestiltskin," but I had to wear a wig because, as everyone knows, princesses don't have short hair. I always had.

Would I have really offed myself if I didn't have a show to look forward to? Impossible to say, because I kept getting cast. So, with the paper route, babysitting and the theater, I must've looked like a real go-getter. Ha. Now look at me.

TWENTY

It's a good thing I was flush with cash, because it was around this time that my dad lost his job. It had something to do with a bad loan to his buddy, but he asserted that it was an excuse to replace him with a woman for half the price. Who knows what the real story was, considering my father's penchant for untruths told for the purpose of self-preservation. He was involved in the Chamber of Commerce and Kiwanis, local men's organizations with unspecified duties. It's likely that, through these groups, the cronyism that riddles national governments asserts itself on a local level via trickle-down treachery.

All was not lost, see, because Dad was also selling baseball memorabilia. He'd amplified his boyhood collection with every edition from every year following. For those of you who are fortunately unfamiliar, there aren't just Topps cards, you know. There are Donruss and Fleer brands too, and a collector needs each and every one, from every year. It was a big business then, as big as the full-wall length closet he constructed to contain his collection. These were the Reagan years, a boom time. Some guys did coke, other guys did baseball cards and boats. We'd actually had a boat when I was very young, but my mom became terrified that something awful would happen. I get that from her, I always think something awful's gonna happen. I call it Worst Case Scenario Syndrome. It has many sufferers.

When dad came in and told us he'd lost his job, apparently I got up and hugged him, told him we'd be okay. Mom told me it was nice that I did that, but I don't remember doing it at all.

Dad was offered a job at another bank at the same salary, but turned it down. Baseball cards were doing pretty well, so he was going to focus on that for a while. He would go away for whole weekends to baseball card shows, and sometimes I would work with him at the local ones. I even kind of got into it. I randomly got a Ryne Sandberg error card in a wax pack, which was worth 50 bucks right away, so that's pretty exciting stuff. Plus, I have all these pictures of me with aged baseball players whose accomplishments I did not appreciate at the time, but whose names stick with me and give the illusion that I know what I'm talking about on occasion.

Eventually, baseball was the only thing dad would talk to me about. I understand that he was grateful for the common ground, and I'm sure that's why I got into it in the first place, but boy, did I get sick of it. His ceaseless droning infuriated me, and one day I finally burst out angrily that I didn't care about any of it. As though it weren't obvious, I informed him that I wasn't a boy. Right after I said it, I noticed that the song "I'm Not a Boy" by Book of Love was playing on WDRE. Maybe it had subconsciously informed my outburst...or maybe my outburst had informed the programming, maybe I was somehow connected to the universe, I thought. It certainly seemed more likely than any connection to my father. He wasn't very good at communicating with me. Well, with anyone, really. He would later try to cheer me by mowing my name into the lawn of the backyard. I thought that was pretty weird.

The administration of the school saw me floundering. You have to hand it to them, they must have seen what was happening to me, and they reached out in the only way they could. The principal and vice principal brought me before the Board of Education. They gave me an award, acknowledging my grades and community theater work, plus I was still in the communications club and the debate club now too. I had played French horn in All-County, which was an honor, sure, but I swear to you that I was awful. It just so happened that I was one of two French horn players in the county. I tooted atonally, always several notes behind. I lacked dexterity, and froze, just like with tap dancing and multiplication. I marveled at the melody emanating from the first chair horn player. I couldn't do what she was doing. I was a joke. That's all I could think as the adults on the Board oohed and aahed at my list of accomplishments. It was all a load of crap. The pictures show me in the center of an applauding blur, my head bowed, my smile crooked and forced. It felt like a consolation prize, a ridiculous farce. I wished they would stop. I wished it would all stop.

And, you know? I marched in two parades with that damned horn, still overmatched by its size. In the first parade, in addition to our matching used and soiled red wool blazers, I was wearing that long black pencil slim skirt from Lena. A pre-parade jump off the bleachers had split the slit. As I marched along, the tear deepened and I went from slit to slut. By the time I reached the parade's end, I had to turn the breach to the side because it was up to my hip.

There's video evidence of the other parade. We were wearing the same wool blazers, but it was Memorial Day and nearing 90 degrees. So parched was I when I reached my parents watching at the side of the road, that they did not get a home video of my horn playing, no. Rather, they have a reel of me gesticulating wildly for one of them to get me water. I don't know why they didn't. Like everyone else, they probably just laughed at over-dramatic little me. Couldn't they see I was in hell? It was three quarters of the way through the parade with still a half-mile to go. I wasn't going to play anymore in high school. Fuck that noise.

TWENTY-ONE

We got junior high yearbooks. It was the era of big hair and some girls had coifs that exceeded the frame of their photos. My hair wasn't so big in my picture. It was too thin to ever hold the spray and I rued my inability to match up to the style of the day. I went to a carnival with two peripheral friends and no joke, when we got stuck upside down on a roller coaster, they took out their aerosols and started spraying. My hair was scraggly and wild and that's why I cut it short. In my picture I wore a turtleneck with a v-neck sweater and a strained smile.

Almost nobody signed my yearbook. I felt too awkward to even ask anyone to do so. Still-reigning chief tormentor Lance Nardo grabbed my book from in front of me in class. "Here Jaime, I wanna sign yours," he said. I just waited for the inevitable. I saw him present his work to the class, laughing as he threw it back down on my desk. I flipped through to find he'd just scrawled a big mess on the last pages. Whatever. That I could handle.

Before graduation, there was an 8th grade formal. Nobody asked me to be their date, of course. I cried beforehand about my hair, my dress, about nothing being right. I didn't cry at the formal though, which must've been some kind of record. I didn't have any fun either. I was so, so alone.

TWENTY-TWO

Summer was better. Summer always was. Mom was finally letting me go to this horseback riding camp. I'd seen the ad and asked about it for years, but she didn't think I'd really be into it once I got there. She thought it was enough that they had a riding excursion at Driftwood once a week. It wasn't, I assured her. We didn't really have enough money for me to go to camp anymore, but what were the options? Leaving me at home all day for the whole summer while my parents worked, that was a frightening proposition in my state. Idle time was my most malicious foe.

Thomas School of Horsemanship was amazing. A lot of the girls there had their own horses, but they weren't all stuck-up about it. I was in the lowest level class, just walking and trotting, but when I had my show at the end of the summer, all the girls from my group ran out and surrounded me and my dappled loaner horse, Cinnamon, and our red 2nd place ribbon. There's a nice picture of that, with me wearing a smile as big as my helmet. My mom laughed at me, "You always say you don't have friends, and look at that." Yeah, I was surprised by it too. It was really nice. One older girl and I especially bonded over Depeche Mode. We would jump in front of little kids and sing the refrain from "Strange Love." We'd pounce before them and point down in unison, demanding to know of their pain tolerance. That was a pretty strange thing to do, now that I think of it. They would scream and run away. We would laugh.

Carrie moved to California with her boyfriend Graham that summer. The night before she left, mom took us to see Depeche Mode at the Meadowlands Arena, in New Jersey. It was the tour for the Violator album and we were in the 23rd row. I stood on my chair and screamed the whole time, so much that the guy in front of me complimented my lungs. It didn't strike me until later that he may not have been appreciative. He could've just said to shut up. I'm glad he didn't, I was having a good time. This music had given me so much. In it, I found comfort and understanding. Here were my saviors, right before my eyes, flawlessly singing the songs that elucidated my pain and kept it from being solitary. Mom and Carrie stood on their chairs and cheered right by my side. It was great. In my infinite thrift, I got two bootleg t-shirts in the parking lot for the price of what one cost at the merch booth. I'm surprised I didn't get a talk from Carrie about how this copyright infringement was a slight to the artist I so admired. Morals gain such flexibility in the monetary realm.

So, I entered high school a bit of an alterna-chick. I was still skewing preppie, but we were all living under the spell of The Gap at the time. I ran for 9th grade president, but only because literally nobody else was. Nothing I'd done to this point mattered, on a transcript level. My record from here on is what counted, and so, I became 9th grade president. I had to keep my record up to get into a good college. I'd always figured that I would go to Yale. Yale Drama School, I'd asserted since elementary school, but I didn't really think about it much at all anymore. I'd always been such a big planner, but now I just focused on getting through the day at hand.

There were no more enrichment classes in high school. The program was unfortunately and inexplicably terminated, but I was still on the "accelerated" track. Us types were mixed in with resentful, slower 10th graders, which made the "honors" classes seem much more of a detriment than any kind of honor. Due to alphabetic misfortune, seated to my rear in Biology class was one Charlie Beltram. He was an example of what happened to kids with ADD before they started giving out Ritalin. Charlie saw the bulls-eye on my head right off, and he had a super vantage point from which to take his shots. My unopposed election resulted in a steady stream of quiet mock reverence, murmured from behind.

I woke up hysterical on Halloween morning, suddenly convinced that, as president, I had to wear a costume to school. My poor accommodating mother tore through the house to find something, desperate to calm me, to please me. I know it's ridiculous. It was Halloween, what's the big deal? Everything always seemed like such a big deal, and everything sent me into paroxysms of anxiety. Wonder where I got that trait from? However, my dad lashed out with his anxiety, while mine devoured me from within.

I'd gotten much taller, fast enough that I had stretch marks on my hips. I'd gotten so tall, in fact, that my father's local softball league uniform was not terribly ill fitting. We had a winner! I went to school anxious as hell, embarrassed for myself, and amongst the very few people wearing costumes. I tensed up as I walked into 3rd period bio and Charlie took aim. As I sat down, the cooing began. "Oh, look at the little baseball player, isn't she *cute*? Awww, hey! Hey, baseball player, where's your bat," and on and on. And on. I just hung my head and cried.

Other than Charlie, I really liked bio. It was interesting and our teacher was an excited little Muppet of a lady. That's one of the last times I remember paying attention, in that class. Phylum and xylem and all of that. My favorite was the story of how they used to get rid of tapeworms before modern medicine. Turns out they'd starve you for a few days, then put a piece of salted meat on your tongue. Smelling this food that they had been deprived of, the tapeworm would COME UP THROUGH your esophagus and into your mouth to snatch the meat, and the doctors would grab that worm and PULL IT OUT. Sometimes it would slip from their hands and retreat back into you and you'd have to do it all over again. I don't know how people lived back then. I barely know how they do now, when things are so easy, so convenient. I wonder if there was depression in those days, or if it is a byproduct of our leisure time. Life was so much more difficult then, it seems to me that just the work necessary to live would be distraction enough from any mental distress.

I broiled with fury over my easy life that seemed so hard. My English teacher had a competition in which we had to say the past Presidents' names, in order, as fast as we could. I refused, it having nothing to do with English. It felt like it was a cruel circus game, an abuse of his tenured power. Mostly, though, I knew I couldn't win. Just like tap-dancing or multiplication or French horn fingering, I would get flustered. Too much pressure. Talking fast, I'd stammer, my mind would seize. I hated that teacher. He was condescending and chauvinistic. I started hating teachers a lot. I hated them a lot more than I didn't, and it became impossible for me to learn if I did not respect my teacher. I'd spend the class bristling at their every word. I stopped making honor roll right away.

I caught the attention of the other outcasts, kids in black with scruffy hair. Two of the girls, reticent to allow a dilettante into the circle, quizzed me first on various alternative rock topics. I knew some of the answers, and hoped it was enough. I was keenly aware that most people in the world just made friends and stayed that way, and that it was certainly turning out differently for me. I don't know why they made me jump through hoops. There were other chicks in the circle who couldn't pass that kind of test. They probably didn't have to take one, even.

So, I had friends now. We ate lunch together. Finally, I had a destination again. There were five or six girls, all a year older than me. My wardrobe darkened to match theirs. We sat at the table with two senior "freak" guys. That's what we were called…freaks. Mac Hennessey lived in the boys' home near my house, but was as harmless and gregarious as you wouldn't expect a young man to be in those circumstances. He had a thin braided tail down to his ass, as long as his whole head of hair used to be. The other one was Corey Alton whom I had a giant crush on. He had tinted red hair and was clearly on the road to gaydom, a trait that made him all the more alluring to me. I am so drawn to the unattainable.

Mac and Corey didn't hang out with us outside of school at all. Although, once Corey did ask to borrow my black and white striped socks to wear to a party. Of course, I let him. At least my socks would get to hang out with him. When he gave them back, they smelled like they'd been hung to dry in a closet of pot smoke. I knew what the smell was. Mom had taken me to enough concerts to know that. When I was almost caught taking pictures of The B52s from our 8th row seats, I pointed the guard, instead, to the pot smokers down the aisle. Cruel of me, perhaps, but I had disdain for them. Mom told me that what they were doing was wrong.

Having forged no faculty partnerships on the high school level, I brought the socks over to the junior high health teacher, Mr. Goodman. I wanted to talk to him. I needed his guidance, his empathy that I had once felt. I was reaching out. I asked him if he thought the socks smelled like pot and he said they did. He didn't ask why I had come. He didn't ask what was going on with me. I had come for answers, for help. He didn't tell me to stay away from that guy. He seemed nervous. He didn't tell me anything.

There was no immediate cause for concern, though, since, as I mentioned, we didn't really hang out with Corey and Mac. My girls and I, despite our outward disdain of the popular crowd, went to their parties. We drank.

Boy, did we drink.

TWENTY-THREE

It was during spring break. I didn't like beer, but I drank it. Lots of it and fast. It was my first time at the bleachers, where everyone hung out on weekend nights. You could walk on a shady path between there and the local 7-11. It was quite the social circuit. It was my first time really drunk.

Suddenly this 11th grader was talking to me. He was wearing a football jacket and he was beautiful. Dark brown hair with blue, blue eyes. I kid you not that he shared his name with a certain infamous woman killer. It was spelled differently, but they had similar life trajectories, I imagine. He was holding beers and I asked for one. He said he'd give me two if I gave him a blowjob. I didn't agree to the trade, but eventually we wandered off together. We stumbled down the path behind the bleachers, and ambled through the fields, kissing. We fell and writhed until he stood up and unzipped his pants. I'd never given head before. He said something to the effect that it was hard to believe, though whether that was inspired by my prowess or my willingness, I'm not certain. I stopped and said this wasn't right, that we weren't even going out.

"Do you wanna go out?" he asked. "Yeah,' I said, and continued with my charge. I swallowed him. I didn't know what else to do. "She swallowed it," the N.W.A. song said, further requesting that my teeth not be involved.

I stood up and then I heard it. Applause. Our stumbling had led us to the middle of the soccer field, in clear view from the back of the bleachers. I laughed with embarrassment, drunkenness. I bowed.

My friends appeared from out of nowhere. "What are you guys doing?' I asked. "I think we should ask what YOU'RE doing.' Gina spit back, just like I hadn't. A cloud of shock and shame hung over them. I laughed. "It's okay," I said, "we're going out."

Gina was turning out to be my best friend. She lived down the block from the school and it was easy to stay at her house after nights like these. And there were more.

First, however, I had to deal with the repercussions from this one. When I woke up, the shame I'd lacked the night before was as apparent as the blackened string of hickies on my neck. It looked like a map of the Hawaiian Islands. It being Spring Break, the next day back in school was not for another week, thankfully. Steve and I talked on the phone, awkwardly pretending that we had some sort of actual relationship. I suppose that it was pretty honorable of him to make the effort.

I was cat sitting for the people I baby-sat for while they were on vacation. How better to cement my newfound union than by having a rendezvous in the Shenkman's Jacuzzi? I didn't know how to turn it on. We filled it up and got in, naked and uncertain. We groped feebly, halfheartedly. I wanted to leave. We used the Shenkman's towels, which I folded up damp and put back in the closet. I didn't dry out the Jacuzzi. They must've known, but nobody ever said anything. Of course, they didn't ask me to babysit anymore, either. No big deal, I still had other families that somehow trusted me with their children.

I went to school late the next Monday. Had trouble getting out of bed for some reason. Can't imagine why. When I walked into 2nd period English class, Bobby Perillo exclaimed only "Andrews!," and in doing so expressed the sum of the shocked and mocking thoughts of everyone in that room. Possibly even the president-pumping pig of a teacher. Thus, the crying began, but I knew the worst was to come. All through bio, Charlie Beltram chanted, "hummer... hummer..." I had never heard that phrase before, but I had a pretty good idea of what it meant. What's more is, it turned out the story that was going around was that I'd done it for two beers. It wasn't true.

I never got any beer. Would that have been worse? At least I'd have gained something in the transaction.

It had already been hard enough to raise my head in the hallways. Now when I did, I was met with disgusted glares and whispers. I called Steve and said it wasn't going to work out, our "relationship." Who were we trying to kid?

The pressure on me was partially alleviated when, a couple of months later, Steve wandered off with yet another drunk girl. He was stopped that time and from then on was considered a bit of a predator. Something about guys with that name must be hard-wired as woman-haters, I guess. They didn't look dissimilar, either, my paramour and his infamous name-sharer. If someone told me that the recipient of my first fellatio would eventually go on to kill a bunch of chicks, I'd not be too surprised. It's pretty hard to surprise me, though. I know that anything can happen. It usually does, too.

TWENTY-FOUR

I did not retreat into solitude, no, I continued on my rampage. Gina had stolen a bottle of vodka from her parents, and we added some Jello mix in an attempt to dilute its strength. Actually, it was just as strong, but now it tasted like berry-flavored poison. I couldn't feel its impact as I continually slugged away. It was a big party that night and everyone was hanging out at the local pool. The pool was cordoned off, but there was talk of scaling the 20-foot fence that surrounded it. Nobody dared. Even I, in my increasing inebriation, wouldn't risk it, though I clearly had a growing predilection to doing whatever dumb thing that crossed my mind. This night, I had my sights set on Mark Lanzer. Still, he would not yield to me. I sat next to him on a bench. We talked as I tried to hold my head together. It spun and spun.

The next thing I knew, I was on the ground, flailing in my own bright-pink vomit. I was barely conscious. I had the brilliant idea of bringing a camera with me that night, and it was taken from my bag. It was used to photograph me there, prostrate and filthy, while the different young men in attendance pulled down their pants and put their asses or balls in my face. I heard faraway laughter. I was oblivious.

An older guy that I didn't even know told my friends he'd get me out of there. I was lucky that he had the honest intention of transport, a particularly noble feat considering my constant spewing and his vintage Firebird. I was thrown in the back with a bag for my waste and driven home. He carried me to my door and rang the bell. It was after midnight. My parents came to the door, thanked the mysterious gentleman and shepherded me, stumbling to the bathroom for more expulsion. "I'm sorry," I slurred. My mom cried. My dad laughed. Kids will be kids, after all. Gina begged me to get the film developed, seeing as how it held images of the nether regions of our school's elite. I refused. Nobody's ass was worth seeing myself that way.

I'd wind up being able to offer descriptions of most of what was revealed in those shots anyway, as they each eventually turned to me for their oral needs. There was Phil Leach, sexy, dirty and stupid, whom I took in the drainpipe of the sump next to the school, and who once told me he had fucked the roast beef in the deli in which he worked. Charming! My taste was unparalleled.

Then there was Nathan O'Neal. He was easily the hottest guy in school, with his floppy raven hair and grey-green eyes. Each member of his family were cut from a magical mold, the seeming progeny of Clark Kent, and their names all started with the letter 'N.' His sister Niara or something was a beauty queen hopeful in my sister's class. She won Miss Hawaiian Tropic and was featured, unflatteringly, in a documentary about how creepy Levittown is. They showed her vacantly waving in slow motion as she espoused her lofty dreams of being lauded as beautiful.

Nathan approached me at a keg party. We played some stupid mating game that included us "talking" by knocking our heads against each other's shoulders. I swooned. Nathan O'Neal, talking to me. Touching me. He pulled me aside. "Look," he said, "I just want to be with you, I don't want to go out or anything." Of course! Anything! You had to admire his forthrightness.

Nathan walked with me to an old local cemetery, where we laid down amongst the dead. I didn't even finish him off. I was bored. Our union wasn't lit by any torrid fire. I was just going through the motions, doing what I was supposed to do. I gave him my black choker and one of my anc earrings -- offerings on the altar of a teenage god. When my mother came to pick me up later, he walked me to her car. "Whoo! He's hot!" she said as we pulled away. Quite an accomplishment. Gina called me the next day wondering what the hell happened, hoping that I had had sex with him. She thought him worthy of my virginity, just because of how he looked, who he was.

Yeah, I'm still a virgin, clinically speaking, though it seems I remain in this state mostly because nobody sticks around long enough to take it to that level. Not that I would hold out so long, but certainly longer than the one-night span of my current unions. I have some standards.

Clearly, I'm not going to find a soul mate amongst my schoolmates, not when I've already made myself a punch line. I mean, just look at this desk. I sit here, staring at its slurs, and can't help but dread what is to come.

TWENTY-FIVE

There's this concert coming this summer, Lollapalooza, and it sounds to me like the opening to the gates of Utopia. Not just the great bands playing, but also the promise of a giant field of people who like the same things as me. Who could maybe, then, like me too. I have to go. Thankfully, Anne Raymond's older sister and her boyfriend offered - or were forced to - take our crew along with them. The show is two hours away in the wilds of New Jersey, so we're going to camp out the following night. I'm going to share a tent with Gina. It's going to be amazing.

I put a temporary black dye in my hair before the show. I guess I want to distinguish myself further? Funny how you can do that by making yourself more like something else. I'm bucking conformity only to adhere to a more stringent subset of it. Still, amongst my gaggle of barely teen-aged girls, I'm attracting no suitors. Usually my good time is dependent on such a thing, but the music, the atmosphere, it's phenomenal. The rain starts coming down and black rivulets of temporary dye are streaming down my neck, but this guy next to me hands me his t-shirt to use as a turban. He's not laughing at me. He is literally giving me the shirt off his back. Where are these people to be found in the everyday? I feel right at home. These are my people.

When we get back to the campground, Anne's sister lets us have some beer. There are a group of young guys camping next to us, and we drink with them by the fire. The only one that could be considered cute, even by firelight, peels off with Anne. Anne always hooks up, she's adorable in that way that guys like, long hair and laughy.

Everyone goes to sleep. It's so dark. There's only one other guy left awake with me. He starts to kiss me and I oblige, noticing in the fire's light that he is horrible looking. Like a monster. To me, anyway. His fish mouth opens to swallow me, and his hands reach for my sad little breasts as he pushes his crotch against mine. I don't bear it long before I tell him that I'm tired, and crawl into my tent next to Gina. I can't sleep at all on the cold hard ground, but when he calls to me the next morning before leaving, I pretend that I've never slept more deeply.

TWENTY-SIX

Mom and I are in California visiting Carrie. We do a quick tour of Los Angeles (it seems awfully seedy) before heading down for a day at Disneyland. The happiest place on earth is not contagious.

There's some Disney employee talking to a group of us, doing crowd work. He targets me and asks where I'm from. "Long Island," I reply. He moves on, muttering, "poor rich kid," infuriating me. I'm not rich at all. I mean, I guess I am, when compared to kids in Bangladesh, but otherwise, no. I don't know why it makes me so mad. It doesn't seem like a Disney-approved riff.

Mom takes a picture of me and Carrie. We look awkward, a pair of black-clad dorks in a candy-colored pseudo-paradise.

We then head north to where Carrie goes to school, in Santa Barbara. It's beautiful, but I'm depressed, what else is new? I always feel like I'm walking through invisible sludge.

The apartment where Carrie lives with Graham seems alluringly illicit. It smells of youthful independence, and I'm drawn to the giant Ministry skull poster on the wall.

Material Issue is playing at the venue in the center of town, Anaconda. I really dig their song, "Valerie Loves Me." I trot out my trusty black and white striped tights and crush myself to the front of the crowd, as is my wont.

After the show, I'm approached by a young woman who asks if I want to meet the band. She takes me up the stairs to the green room, my mother in tow. She isn't stupid. Why is this chick delivering 14-year-old girls to these louche-looking men, lazing post-show on this dingy sectional?

Whatever their original intentions were, they settle on signing a poster for me, and I am ecstatic. One of the guys draws stripes on his leg and writes, "wrap those legs around me." I guess that was their original intention. I kinda wish my mom wasn't with me.

We drive back to the airport with me lying down in the back seat, despondent. I'm listening to the new Depeche Mode. It's good, but has become really popular already. That's annoying. I want to keep everything to myself.

Back at home, I am going to see lots of concerts. With little else to be financially responsible for, tickets are the chief expenditure of my varied job proceeds. Because my friends are a year older, mom's comfortable letting me go with them to shows, even into the city. She just wants me to be happy. I'm still not.

I spend $150 to see Morrissey front row center. Posters of the self-proclaimed messiah of misanthropes have replaced those of Depeche Mode on my walls. Depeche Mode is misery-lite. They don't nearly capture the melancholy levels of Morrissey and The Smiths...and they're so damn popular now.

It's the advent of the compact disc. Jesus, am I supposed to replace all my tapes now? The first one I buy is "Louder than Bombs." The warbled words are as funny as they are sad. The Smiths are the latest musical interpretation of my pain, and I find solace in their songs. It is hard to say whether or not the dour lyrics improve upon or compound my torment. On the one hand, I don't feel so alone and misunderstood. On the other, I have an increased vocabulary of malcontent, a thousand-fold battle cry for my own private war.

At the show, people are bounding over the barrier to join Moz on stage. Naturally, I do the same, during "Sing Your Life." He's reclining behind a speaker as my gangly, bespectacled frame leans over him, wearing a shirt emblazoned with his face and those black and white striped socks that I love. Love as much as I love this man whom I am now hovering over.

I burst into tears.

"Everything you say, all your words, mean so much –" is what I manage to blurt out before I'm grabbed in a headlock by a security guard, lifted into the air and unceremoniously dumped on the wings of the stage. A fey young man, with blonde hair shaped into our musical host's style, is deposited alongside me – having also just shared a Moz moment – and we hug and weep in exaltation before wending our way back through the masses to our seats.

At a concert, I can leave my body. I become something greater: part of a mass of rapturous souls.

At home, I listen over and over to the saddest of songs. My poor parents know that the way to my heart is through my ears, and come to my bedroom door with "The Queen is Dead." They look through concerned and hopeful eyes, desperate to find an easy ointment to soothe my pain. It works too. I am so, so happy to get this new addition to my small collection. I'm thankful. For only 12.99, my parents had purchased a night without crying.

TWENTY-SEVEN

I'm in 10th grade now. My headaches are gone, but they have been replaced with screaming fits of purely emotional suffering. My mom vacillates between trying to help me, and hiding in her room, herself overwhelmed by my pain. When she does come to me, sometimes I strike at her and scream for her to go, only to long for her return. I still cut myself, but more surreptitiously so as to avoid detection. When trying on swimsuits, Mom busts me for the cross I etched between my stupidly small breasts the week prior. I'm not religious or anything, it had just seemed like a freaky sort of dramatic thing to do.

So, Mom and dad take me to South Oaks, the local mental hospital, for an intake evaluation. I want to go away. I don't care about anything. I just want to die. Everything that was good in me has turned to shit and I can't see the use of going forward. They tell me to go home and think about whether I'd like to spend some time there, and get the help I so clearly need. The concept is pretty daunting. "I'm not crazy. Institutionalized. You're the one who's crazy. Institutionalized." That's on the punk rock mixtape my sister made for me. A mental hospital. Do I really want that stigma? I figure it can wait a bit. I can figure this out.

TWENTY-EIGHT

In a school photography class, I show promise with composition, but refuse to expend any effort beyond the actual taking of pictures. I make some sloppy attempts at developing and mounting my shots but am infuriated by their lack of perfection. So, I decide to coerce other classmates to do that work for me. I'm just the most spoiled brat.

There's a senior in the class who'd been left back. Andy is a longhaired skater guy who gives me a hard time, but in a way that seems to be friendly enough. He asks me if I want some acid. Seems he has a bunch.

Ummm, sure, why not? I don't need peer pressure. He didn't call me chicken or force me to do anything. If something is offered, I want it. Gina and I plan to split it in two and drop our halves at the local teen goth club, Hotel Leningrad. We've been going there every week. I go and mosh like a maniac with guys twice my size to songs as furious as I am. This congregation of the alienated feels like heaven to me, like a concert but cozier. So there I am for my 15th birthday, tripping out for the first time. Gina and I giggle around the bar confusedly. We lose Anne, who is dressed skimpily, and as I walk around the bar I ask a tall, skinny boy in a Ministry shirt if he's seen a girl in short shorts with thigh-highs.

"No," he says, "If I had I would've followed her.'

"Typical!" I blurt at him and start away. They always love Anne. He follows after me and apologizes for what he said. Any resentment I have melts away in his blue eyes. We sit against the wall and talk all night, getting up occasionally to dance or, rather, hurl ourselves into the people around us. It's time to go home. He writes his number on a napkin alongside the words, "I hope you remember me." His name is Jason.

Gina and I go back to her house. Still wired, we take the

trek to 7-11 in the middle of the night. The Arab music playing inside drills into the recesses of our brains, and picks at the chords of our nerves. We dance with a cardboard Frankenstein from a Halloween display, and we both decide to buy cigarettes. Still no peer pressure, it just seems like a good idea. Simultaneously. Cigarettes are cool. We're so cool. We walk back to her house, wondering if that which is shining down on us through the fog is God, or just a streetlight. When we get home, we put on "Clockwork Orange" and blow our little minds.

The next day is the homecoming game. We haven't slept, we haven't showered, and we haven't ever, ever been to a school-based sporting event before, but we think maybe it'll be fun to show up. They bring Nathan O'Neal onto the field. A couple of weeks prior he'd flown off the side of a mountain in a skimobile accident and broken both of his legs. He was lucky that was all the damage done, apparently. The crowd roars as he's wheeled out, waving. The crowd is chanting his name. Nathan doesn't even play football. "Oh, to be a teenage messiah,' I drawl to Gina, my voice stained by decadence.

TWENTY-NINE

I call Jason the next day and he calls me back while I am baby-sitting. It's the last couple in the neighborhood that trust me with their kids. They're awake when I take the call and stand outside to have a cigarette while I talk to him. The kids stand in the doorway pointing at me, their mouths agape, totally scandalized that I am doing what all the teachers say you're not supposed to. Jason and I make a plan to meet next week back at Hotel Leningrad. I spend the week elated, on air. I start writing Jaime & Jason all over my books next to The Smiths, Ministry, Skinny Puppy and Christian Death. I am never asked to babysit again. Not for them, not for anyone.

That's fine, I have other means of support. Each one of my friends and I take jobs at the mall doing surveys. Those annoying people with clipboards asking for a minute of your time? That's us. We make you smell some perfume and ask if it makes you feel apathetic, dull and sluggish. That is actually one of the options. The whole job makes me feel apathetic, dull and sluggish. It really couldn't be a worse field for me, hating as I do to foist myself on others and be rejected by them, and yet, I certainly seem to gravitate toward just that sort of vulnerable scenario. What is acting, after all, but a steady stream of foisting and rejection?

There is one really nasty boss. We hate each other but she can't get rid of me because I am too effective at wrangling suckers for questioning.

This bitch's mom has just died and we're all eating lunch around the table in the company break room. They're talking about the burial. I say that I don't want to be buried when I die, I just want to rot. Gina kicks me under the table. I didn't mean to be cruel, I just don't think sometimes. In fact, if there is something that isn't supposed to be said, you can pretty much count on me to come out with it.

THIRTY

When I see Jason again, he is cuter than I remember. Seventeen, 6'3" and painfully thin with those warm blue eyes and a baby face. He's wearing a frayed Notre Dame hat and a t-shirt with a long- sleeved shirt underneath. He's a skater guy. Those are my favorite kind of guys! I am immediately in love. He asks if a girl like me would consider going out with a guy like him. What is a girl like me? Who the fuck am I? Of course I would.

I have a boyfriend! My first real boyfriend. I write our official date, 11.1.91, all over my books next to our names. It is so numerologically appealing! I tell everyone about him. The girls in my classes ask for pictures, like they don't believe me since he doesn't go to our school.

Jason lives in a super-posh area, but in an apartment with his mom, who is a divorced school bus driver. My mom regularly takes the half hour drive to get me over there for our make-out sessions. Is it crazy of her? Over-indulgent? You see your daughter smiling after weeks of screaming and see what kind of choices you make.

Dates with Jason are listening to music and sometimes drinking 40's with his friends. It's now the third week of our relationship and he's at my house while my parents aren't home. After the recent honing of my oral skills with any lucky loser that showed me attention, Jason becomes the first to reciprocate. I feel numbness and tingling behind my eyes, then it spreads through every limb as I shake. I cry out. I don't realize that this is an orgasm. I know only that I love the man who makes me feel this way. I am altered.

My dad comes home soon after and I startle when I see him in the hall. He asks me something but I can't hear him. I realize that I'm acting like I'm on drugs. I feel like I am on drugs. Love is the drug I'm thinking of.

THIRTY-ONE

South Oaks calls to follow up on my intake evaluation, see if I am still considering hospitalization. I don't need that crap anymore, I told mom...I have a boyfriend!

It being a busy era of new experiences, I try pot too. My mom got me tickets to see Red Hot Chili Peppers with my friends in the city. The show is at the Roseland Ballroom and the openers are Smashing Pumpkins and Pearl Jam. We arrive during Pearl Jam. Nobody pays attention to them. Nobody knows who they are. As the Pumpkins mesmerize me, a stranger hands me a joint. My friends aren't around. I pull deeply on it, without a second thought.

When the Chili Peppers come on, I rush to the front of the stage and spend the show crushed against the barricade, 10 feet from the men that my sister had been following around SoCal for years. She told me they used to be much cooler before I discovered them. Said they used to wear only socks over their dicks when they played. They were rather unfortunately fully clad at this show. At the end, I catch the drumstick that the drummer throws out. How do drummers throw their sticks into crowds? I bet people really get hurt that way. I don't though, I catch it like a lance thrown by a fellow warrior. It's awesome. My life is amazing.

On the way home, the girls and I compose a song. It sounds not unlike X's "Nausea," which is also on that mix tape of punk music that my sister made for me. I say my friends and I wrote it, but it's all me. I'm always sharing credit when I'm the one to whom it is due.

"You roll over in the morning and he's not next to you.
You think he could at least call, after he slept with you.
He doesn't love you, so you might as well die,

he doesn't love you, so go fuck another guy.
My head is full of memories, my pillow's wet with tears
doesn't even matter now my stomach's full of beers -
inebriation."

It goes on droning like that and ends with a real thrashy
part where you scream "you know you're gone now, you know
you're gone now, you think you're bad now, wait til you - roll
over in the morning." I'm pretty proud of it. I don't know what
I am talking about though. I'm still a virgin, after all. All of my
friends are too, though my time for that is dwindling.

THIRTY-TWO

We're in Ray's basement. Jason's friend. We try, but Jason, he's a pretty big boy, and I am a pretty small girl and we are on a couch. I cry, I can't. It hurts. Jason measures in at a good 8 inches or so. At 17 he's already covered in body hair, poor thing. He is beautiful. He loves me. It just doesn't work.

The next day it does, though, and it's our one-month anniversary. 12.1.91. The two of us smoke cigarettes and laugh and kiss afterwards at his small kitchen table. That becomes a ritual, one during which I am often unnerved. My expectations are too high. I want things to be perfect...why can't they be perfect?

The next time I go to the survey job, my head is going to explode. I have to go see him. It's raining. It's 9 o'clock on a Friday night. If I don't see him immediately, I'm going to freak out. My mom balks but she can see the desperation in my eyes. She takes me over there. His mother is home and we have yet to discover the possibility of quiet lovemaking, so we escape into the night looking for somewhere, anywhere to go. We consider doorways and overhangs, and some shaded areas in the cemetery we sometimes hang out in. We walk to a nearby pier where a building is being constructed. Jason thinks we should check it out, but I am not very optimistic.

He tries the doorknob, and it turns. This brand-new building is just sitting there unlocked. For us. We see an alarm system set up and crawled, perhaps unnecessarily, into a small, carpeted side room. It's going to be a doctor's office.

There is new wall-to-wall Berber, and I get rug burn on the small of my back and my knees. It's only the 2nd or 3rd time we've made love, so I am still bleeding. I bleed all over this brand-new rug. Jason tells me that, when he passes by the next day, there's a rug rolled up in the dumpster outside. I laugh with pleasure, but I don't necessarily believe him.

I don't notice it at first. What reason do I have for mistrusting what he tells me? Actually, it's surprising I don't look upon his tales more skeptically, considering my father's similar proclivity for misinformation. He and Jason are amongst the kind of liars who are hard to pin down. They deceive, not monumentally, but pervasively. They lie to self-aggrandize or cover their asses, and if questioned, one story can follow another, like tissues from a box. I would question a person's ability to mythologize thusly if I had not myself been so capable. Jason's tendency to do so was such that his friends call him Aesop. So many fables.

Due to this penchant of his, I do not think Jason is a virgin when we first make love. On the contrary, he has been with more than 50 women, according to his assertion. I mention this to his friend who doubts openly that it's more than 10, but still, it was more than only me. I am sickened to think myself part of this procession of women, all of whom, surely, were superior. The thought of it destroys me.

I weigh everything Jason says to me and nothing measures up. I don't exactly have the best example of love in my home, so I'm not sure what it is, what we are supposed to do. All I know was, we are supposed to be in love and it doesn't seem like it does in the movies.

THIRTY-THREE

I am in an acting class in school, to which, as you can imagine, I feel vastly superior. There's a show coming up soon, a Cole Porter review. I don't sing much anymore, but I am certainly worthy and capable of wielding at least one tune. The teacher doesn't give me one, though. Miss Rudd is an asshole. It's like she is reliving her adolescent ostracization issues by cozying up to all the popular kids 20 years her junior. She gives songs to all of them.

I suppose I can't blame her. We aren't on the best terms. One day, after a fit of recalcitrance, she tells me that she wants to see me after class. I retort that I look forward to it with orgasmic anticipation. She sends me to the office instead.

The principal asks me what's wrong. I don't know. Nothing is wrong. Everything is wrong. I tell him all I want is a cigarette.

"Do you have any?" he asks.

"No, and I don't have any money," I cry, in honest exasperation. You can call it manipulation if you like, but surely I cannot foresee that the principal is going to give me a couple of bucks and send me to 7-11. If only it were that easy to fix me.

I know that he is just trying to reach out, just trying to help. I am hysterical. I am falling apart. Nobody knows what to do for me. But none of them ever really *communicates* with me. You'd think they'd never felt any negative feelings in their lives before witnessing me in the throes of mine. It isolates me even further. They can't be understanding because they can't understand. I can tell they are scared though. There's power in that.

My mom is furious. What if I was hit by a car while walking across the street to feed my – also lethal - habit? Unfortunately, I wasn't.

I get a note in homeroom the next day to go see the school psychologist. She is frizzy haired and ineffectual. She analyzes me and I analyze her right back. I look at Rorschach blots and wonder if I am supposed to say they look like bats or encroaching madmen so that I can be properly sedated. I want medication. Jason is on medication, why aren't I? I want to go to an alternative school. Jason goes to alternative school, why can't I? She assures me that it isn't the right place for me. I wonder what is.

My mother's birthday is coming up and I go to the mall with my father to get her a present. I get her a wallet or something. The view from my eyes is that of an alien being. Everything around me is artificial and other. I walk in a tin abyss and the sounds echo in my head. I go into Sam Goody to find musical refuge. I stare at the new Ministry concert video.

"Jaime," someone says from behind me. I jump 20 feet into the air. I land, shaking, and turn to them. "Are you okay?", they ask. It's someone from school. It doesn't register who it is. "I'm fine," my voice cracks. The words travel a million miles through the inner recesses of my mind, until they push themselves out through my mouth, crystallize in the recycled mall air and drop to the floor with a thud. "I'm going to get this video."

My father drives home with me wailing and banging my head against the passenger window frame. It doesn't alleviate the pain trapped in there. I know it sounds ridiculous. It is ridiculous. I am still that six-month old baby, hurling myself against the bedroom walls. I have an affliction with no physical form, but the pain is nonetheless intense. It is killing me.

We arrive home only to turn around again. I hear my parents' voices, not knowing if they are addressing me or only each other. I move to the backseat and curl there, fetal, tears and snot streaming down my face. My mom gets in the front seat.

They are taking me to the hospital. The attending psychiatrist sits with us. We are all helpless.

"What do you want to happen, Jaime?"

I just want it to be over. I want to die.

"Would you want to spend a little time at a hospital."

Yeah, sure, why not? It will be different. It will be away. It will not be life as I currently experience it, and therefore could only be better.

"What about Jason?", my mom asks. "I don't care. I say, "I don't care." And I don't, either. I check into South Oaks the next day. It's my mother's birthday. Happy Birthday.

THIRTY-FOUR

They walk me to my ward and put me in the room for new recruits, right behind the nurses' station. They take my shoelaces, lest I should be compelled to hang myself with them. The bathroom mirror isn't a mirror at all, but a piece of reflective steel, to prevent any sort of smashing action. I have a round roommate who listens to Pink Floyd's "On the Turning Away" so frequently that I start charging her a quarter for each play. It's her tape player, she can listen to it whenever she wants, theoretically, but I guess I am the dominant one in this relationship. I always go too far in my roles…when I am the lesser, I simper, and if I rule, I do so tyrannically.

Still, this arrangement comes in pretty handy for the pay phone, of which there are two on the unit, each of them always with a line of three or four malcontents.

The kids range from 14-17 and there are all kinds. Thugs, freaks, geeks and homecoming queens. Well, girls that could be homecoming queens if everyone in their school didn't think they were totally insane. One such girl was really in a bad way. When she is admitted, she becomes my roommate for a while too. Her parents are both psychiatrists and, like many in the field, have clearly chosen the profession to work out their own mental instability. The impact on Lynn was such that she has a look in her eye like she could take a bite out of you at any time.

Right away, Lynn starts freaking out, screaming and thrashing. Someone probably told her she couldn't use the phone or something. It never takes much to set any of us off. We are all stunted children, really. Big, bratty babies. The loudspeaker buzzes, "222 Code Blue." We soon realize that this means someone is really going crazy. As she howls, the rest of us are ushered away as large orderlies in white come rushing into the room. We return later to find Lynn wearing a straightjacket and strapped to the bed, heavily sedated and drooling. I've never actually seen a straightjacket before. I guess there is logic in letting us see her that way. If any part of us had wondered what we had to do to be put in one, just for the experience, seeing Lynn lying there certainly drained the concept of any romance it might have.

The next day Lynn is gone. We were never told the outcome of such moves, so we just assume that she has gone to "flight deck." That's where they put the really serious cases. I don't know what the real name of the ward is, but "flight deck" is a suitable enough moniker, it being the destination for those who have "taken off."

I am not so bad as all of that. I am just awfully sad, is all. Awfully, awfully sad and I don't know why. Were it three centuries prior and someone said I was afflicted by demonic possession, it would've made just as much sense as the biochemical reasoning being laid before me now. I know the person I am, or could be, is vibrant and fun, not this pathetic, hateful and blubbering mess. I hate the shrink I am assigned to. He is corpulent and unkempt. He can't make eye contact through his air of condescension. And this is going to help me? Clearly this guy has far more wrong with him than I do, and he's sitting in judgment of me? He doesn't know my life. He's spent his in schools, learning theories. What the fuck does he know about my reality? He's never even lived. I am certain he hasn't really lived.

They are going to try me on medication - the same kind as Jason's. I line up every day for my little paper cup with my little pink pill. They check our mouths afterward to make certain they've been swallowed. Maybe if I save them up like my vitamins in kindergarten, I can take them all at once and be super-sane.

I try to make nice with the two alternative chicks on the

ward. One is from England, which I think is just the coolest thing ever. I ask her what it's like being from somewhere where everybody loves Morrissey. "Everybody loves Morrissey everywhere," she spits back, disgusted. They warm up to me though. We sit around drawing violent stick figures and I let them borrow the tapes my mom made for me of my favorite CD's. I am lucky my parents attend to me with such loving care. Most don't have time or energy for such things, I imagine. But I don't know what I'd do without my music.

Mom and Dad had brought me my CD's, all marked with my name in Sharpie, but I wasn't allowed to keep them. We could only have children's tape players, them being cordlessly indestructible and all. So, mom made me taped copies, and got me a candy-colored Fisher Price device on which to play them. Whatever Jaime needs. Whatever Jaime wants.

Somehow, we tricked the late-night nurse into playing that "Institutionalized" song by Suicidal Tendencies in the common room one night. That was pretty funny. We listen to Nirvana's "Nevermind" all the time. The album just came out and taps into our teen angst zeitgeist like a tuning fork. Kurt Cobain is the screaming mouthpiece for our fury. You can tell he's just like us.

We are all vegetarians. I picked up an animal rights fetish, due mostly, I imagine, to The Smiths' song "Meat is Murder." I don't know how I manage vegetarianism considering the fact that I hate vegetables. Nor do I know how I withstand my own hypocrisy seeing as how I wear big leather Doc Marten boots. At the hospital, they feed us a vacillating variety of lentils and kidney beans. They were boiled, bland and awful. I never want to see another legume again.

My friends at home have been sending me long, entertaining letters. It's really very nice of them. They are the only people that know where I am. The story we floated around the school was that I had mono. I don't even really know if anyone believes that, or if the truth of my commitment has been unleashed. I do find out that my neighbor has gone around telling people that I've gotten pregnant and run away with Jason. I decide to call her and tell her that I'm in Chicago with him, that we are fine and going to get married. That is pretty funny too. Good times, good times in the loony bin.

All in all, it isn't so bad here. Like a vacation. We have cigarette breaks in the courtyard, movie nights and rudimentary school classes that are about as challenging as paint-by-numbers. Still, not everyone is pleased with the reprieve from reality that has been granted to them. Either that or they are always restless, always looking to be somewhere other than where they are. So, some kids talk about escaping. They make plans to run across the vast lawn to a car waiting on the nearby road. One girl tried it and was promptly overtaken and tackled by an orderly. She didn't have anyone there to pick her up, she had just wanted to see what would happen. After that my friends and I sing as that orderly escorts us, changing the Flash Gordon theme song lyrics to say "he'll catch any one of us, if we try to run from him." I mean, I guess it's from Flash Gordon. I don't know it, but I sing along. Poser.

Then something happens. Probably something stupid I said. I do that. I'm not sure what instigated it, but I know my cadre of captive compatriots doesn't like me anymore. It's just like in real life, but on the accelerated scale of the tempestuous. It's one thing to be ostracized by your average teen, and another altogether to inspire the ire of disturbed young girls. That turns from sad to scary real quick.

I'm allowed to go out on day passes now. You're not supposed to have sex on a day pass, and you are searched for drugs when you get back. I don't try the latter but I certainly do the former. It had been two weeks that I'd been hospitalized without Jason. We talk every night and, for a 17-year old with a girlfriend in a mental hospital, he is the height of understanding. On my free day, mom gets Jason and my friends together at my house. They bring me Manic Panic to dye my hair a vibrant fuchsia, and Jason and I re-shave each other's heads, so romantic. I only have hair on the crown of my head, see. It's shaved around the sides and back. I feel like such a bad ass. It is really a very lovely day.

And though I don't bring back drugs, I do carry back a rather nasty urinary tract infection. If you've had it severely you know that it is one of the most painful, discomfiting feelings imaginable. I've always had trouble with them. I remember myself at about seven, pouring water down there to cool the burning. Adding sexual activity, particularly with such a sizable young man, does not help the matter.

My return also unleashes an anger that I hadn't provoked since I was beaten up at Lee Elwin's birthday party. One of those girls, my former friends - Kiera- has purple hair, and apparently my new pink hue was too similar for her to bear. "It's pink," I whimper as they snipe, "P…p is for purple, p is for poser." Maybe I am a poser. Who the fuck isn't? And the people who submerge themselves most deeply in a scene? The ones that know the most about it? I think they're probably the biggest posers of all. Trying so hard as they are. But here I am in my attempt to escape reality, dealing with the same issues I'd been escaping from. We play kickball in our 'gym' class and princess purple pants hurls the ball at my head, hard. I cry in my perceived and perplexing persecution, and am sent back to the ward. As I sit playing the Tetris-like arcade game there on the ward alone, I stiffen when the rest of the kids return. Kiera comes in screaming, "I'll kill her!" I do not turn around as I hear the unmistakable sound of her hitting the floor as she is tackled just steps behind me. I just kept crying and playing the game. I beat the high score.

My therapy is going nowhere. I write long letters to my friends and dark, silly poetry, including one about killing myself on my wedding day.

> "on the day i'm to be wed,
> my dress once white,
> now deepest red,
> to my surprise my sickly groom,
> stands in shock across the room,
> 'what's gone on you've stained your dress?
> we must postpone a week, more or less.'
> 'you silly fool, what do you think?
> these stains are blood and not mere ink,
> i do not love you, i never did,
> i won't be your wife or have your kid,
> so get it through your stinking head,
> for, a minute from now, i will be dead.'"

Cheery stuff. Where does something like that come from when you're fifteen?

THIRTY-FIVE

My chronic symptoms of UTI result in my doctor ordering a pelvic exam, for which, at my age, they need parental consent. My doctor asks me if I'd had sex on my day pass. I admitted I had. He wanted me to tell my mother that this was the reason I needed an exam. No way. No way.

My mother visits and sits with me at a table on the ward and my disgusting, malformed shit of a shrink lumbers over to us.

"For reasons she'd rather not tell you, we want to give Jaime a pelvic exam," he says. I scream, enraged, "you fucking asshole, why don't you just tell her?" Mom's face drains of blood and fills with apprehension. "Tell me what?" she asks. "Jason and I had sex, okay?" Not just my mother, but also the entire visiting room learns of my dalliance that day.

Mom pauses. She says she knew that this was coming, but didn't know it would be so soon. So soon. Why doesn't she just call me a whore? And pretty weird that I had to be sent away not 10 days after my first time. It *was* too soon. I am too young. I am too sensitive. I am too confused and needy. The worst thing a girl like me can do in this situation is to seek sense of self and satisfaction from a guy, but that's the first thing we all do, and nobody is ever there to stop us. All of us with distant daddies just trying to get love any way we can. I hate to make excuses but that's just the way it is.

Mom starts smoking again too. She hadn't smoked since her first divorce, but the strain of the situation is too much for her. Now we smoke together. I can smoke in the house, too, when I'm there.

I get to go home on a day pass for Christmas, and to Jason's too. I have mom buy him combat boots and Calvin Klein's Eternity cologne on my behalf. That's what he wears and I love it so much. I'm always breathing deeply of him and want to continue to do so. He knows I've outdone him in the gift department. It wasn't intentional; I am simply excessive in all regards and want to shower him with whatever he wants. He gives me lipstick. A box of 6 fucking lipsticks in gold cases with a fake jewel set in each of them. Only one of the colors is even decent. Clearly his mother had picked it out for him, if she'd even picked it out. More likely she picked it out of a grab bag at her holiday party with all the other school bus drivers and pawned it off on me. He feels badly about it. I know he does, because he equivocates instantly. "Those cases are real gold," he says.

Sure they are. The paint starts chipping almost immediately.

THIRTY-SIX

I am still in the hospital on New Year's Eve. "Dead Poet's Society" is on TV and it is, naturally, one of my favorites. One might think it not the best viewing choice for suicidal teens; alas, here they are screening it in the level 2 lounge, for patients almost at the end of their treatment. I have not made it to that level yet, but apparently my plea to avoid the main ward's insipid Top-40 ball-dropping show is level-headed enough to warrant a level 2 bolster for the evening.

Kiera and her English cohort had reached that wing by now, and resent my presence vocally. How very advanced of them. I would think by level 2 they'd have learned some level of acceptance. It's a horrible night. I call Jason at midnight. Of course, he isn't home.

When we do talk, I promise him that I will be out soon, but he is at the end of his rope. I don't blame him. A month in your teens is like a year for a dog. I think it's because each day is a greater percentage of your life at that point. As you get older, days are more fleeting because they are an ever-decreasing portion of the time you've already passed.

My sister is home from California for the holidays, and so she's there for the family counseling session we have. It has to be the first time that my mother, father, sister and myself were in a room together since we stopped going out for Red Lobster when I was ten. Once, when we were there, a waitress remarked, "What a happy family." We may have all snorted in response. We were always good at putting up a front like that. Nobody would mistake us for a happy family in this moment. As I sit and predictably weep, my mother and sister tell of the distance between my father and the rest of us. The new shrink I've been given (since I refused to speak to the last one) asked Dad how he felt about this. I've never heard how my father feels about it, being this enemy faction in his own home. He says he wants to work things out. Mom and Carrie say they don't really see the point.

They ask how this makes me feel. I cry, I cry. Surprise, surprise. I say I don't know. I just want everything to be okay. I guess I want everything to be perfect. Or at least more close to perfect than it is. At least not so awful. We don't talk about feelings in our house. It's no small wonder that I don't know how.

Believe me, I know that in the scheme of the universe I have it easy. I don't know why I can't deal with things that other people handle easily. I honestly don't see how people that have it worse can bear it, seeing as how I can't bear things how they are.

The first medication they tried made me catatonic, so then they tried Prozac. It had just come on the market and was supposed to be a savior. I tell the staff that I like it, but they take me off it anyway. They tell me that I just don't realize that I've been running around like a dervish every night, giddy and bouncing off the walls. That doesn't sound like such a negative thing to me.

So here I am. Nothing is different, nothing is better. As much as I wanted to get in the hospital before is how much I want to get out now. I realize what you have to do to get out of here, and I start playing the game. You have to accept everything gracefully, listen to your superiors, show some hope and will to live. I am getting along pretty well until some bitch nurse takes an attitude with me. It isn't necessarily what you say to me, it's how you say it. Condescension. I hate that. Stupid rules, I hate those too. I go to get something from my room when it is "common area" time, and she won't let me. Nothing infuriates me more than adherence to banal bureaucratic bullshit. I pitch a fit on her and I am told it could keep me from going home. I don't think that is true though, they are just trying to scare me. In actuality, I've been there a month, and that is as much as my parent's insurance will cover.

THIRTY-SEVEN

I am on another planet when I get back to school. It's about time for that Cole Porter review and I am not in it, of course, because I've missed so much school. With Gina's aid, though, I sneak into the back of the chorus line and hold up a cardboard fish for the last number. In a rather ill-advised move, Gina had been given provenance over the name of the ship on stage in that scene. She dubbed it the S.S. HOFNAR. It's an acronym for "hard on for no apparent reason." Nobody else knows but us. We laugh as maniacally as my mental health history would suggest.

Gina and I bake brownies with laxatives in them for the class, but nobody is into them. They probably have us figured out. One day in class, after I have a mole removed, a classmate asks me why there is a bandage on my back. Gina and I tell her that I'd gotten stabbed outside Hotel Leningrad. It seems obvious, so we don't bother to tell her that we are kidding. I guess that's just lying.

We still go to Hotel Leningrad all the time. I go with my friends and meet up with Jason. We slam dance and slow dance. In his arms, I sing along with The Smiths, "To die by your side is such a heavenly way to die." I wish he would sing with me. Always longing for the drama.

I may be a little intense. When, in my basement, he doesn't give me the perfectly script-worthy reply to whatever I've posited, I storm upstairs toward the medicine cabinet where Jason has to apprehend me. He slams me against the wall and the bottle of pills I'd grabbed falls to the ground. That was hot. He consoles me in that moment, but breaks up with me soon after. Can't say I blame him there. Nothing like a girl that threatens suicide whenever you disagree.

I am devastated. It's kind of nice to have an actual reason

to be thus. We'd been together for only three months, during one of which I was hospitalized. I don't know what I expected of him. He won't even talk to me, look at me now. I see him at a concert and he's standing stoically on the other side of the venue. The sight of him almost makes me vomit. I thrash around the pit to try and forget, garnering myself a black eye in the process. The next day a girl in school says, "Oh, you're so funky, look at your yellow eye shadow." That's a bruise from a concert, I say. I feel so hardcore. She is the same girl who had once asked what happened to my cut up arms. I had said it was from a cat, and then immediately said no, it was from a pin in one of my costumes. I'm guessing she was skeptical…these were honors classes after all. She was also the same girl who had been the only one to win that 7th grade contest legitimately. When we pulled out the names of our friends and attempted lovers, she was the one we'd never heard of. Now here, she was the only one showing interest in me. I barely acknowledge her.

THIRTY-EIGHT

Jason broke up with me a month ago. I ask this dirt bag girl I go to lunch with sometimes to steal me some sleeping pills. I steal all the time, so I don't see why I wouldn't just do it myself, unless I am trying to let someone know. Make someone stop me. I just tell her that I am having trouble sleeping, but come on, how stupid can you be?

I wake up one day and can't bear the thought of going to school. I'd rather DIE than go to school. "No," my mom said, "Jaime, come on, you have to go, Jaime. Come on, get up." Her tone is harsh and bites me. She goes into the shower to get ready for her own day. I go into the other bathroom with the bottle of co-opted pills and swallow them. All. Well, almost all. About 78 of 100. I think I'd used a few before to actually sleep. I put the pill bottle in front of my mother's bathroom door for her to find when she exits. Such a pathetic, dick move. I go back into bed. I am really tired.

She bursts into my room shouting, "Jaime, wake up, Jaime, c'mon get up, Jaime." My mother doesn't shout ever. My dad is home too because he still isn't working. Baseball cards aren't doing very well either. Nor am I. They take me to the hospital. Blurs of people in white shove a tube up my nose and down my throat and pump my stomach full of charcoal. The charcoal makes me puke blackness as I come in and out of consciousness.

A girl in my school is in this prom dress catalog. I'm so jealous of her. My mom is sitting at the edge of the hospital bed, looking at the catalogue. I sit up and tell her that Jen Johnson is on page 57. She shows me that she is actually reading the hospital forms. Oops. I fall asleep. I wake up to find this kid that sits in front of me in French class hanging out at the foot of the bed. He is asking where Jen is as he flips through the prom dress catalogue. I sit up to tell him when I realize he isn't there at all. Why would he be? Though, I am clearly obsessed with this girl's catalogue coup. I sleep for almost 24 hours.

But I am fine, I wind up being fine. I ask to talk to Jason when I come to, but my guardians think better of it, thankfully. The hospital's staff psychiatrist visits me and I assure him that I have a new lease on life, I've seen the light. He thinks I should continue seeing him. I hadn't been going to that last shrink, as she was useless. This shrink winds up being really ineffectual too. He eats his dinner during my appointments. I finally complain about it and he stops, but I can always tell that he is just sitting there, pretending to listen and wishing he was eating dinner.

When I get back to school after a couple of days, Gina asks me if I'd tried to kill myself. Really frankly. I answer her in kind. "I knew it," she says. That was it.

Jason's friends sure rallied around me though. Gina and I hang out a lot with his friend Al, who has this sort of pompous intellectual Keanu Reaves-thing going. He is 19. We all get high. We are doing that more often now. We sit in this clearing in the woods by the highway. It's such a relief.

Most of our other friends don't really get high. Rebecca's parents are recovering addicts and Ellen knows enough to realize that she is plenty weird without drugs. The girl paints using her own blood, for crying out loud. We all love music though.

We somehow get our parents to let us camp out all night before The Cure is going to play a general admission show at Nassau Coliseum. I feel like parental permissiveness is becoming a running theme here. Anyway, we are amongst the first in line, and it is quite the adventure. Around 4 am these scary-ass kids arrive, kids that make our scary-asses look tame. They push their way up the line that had accrued behind us and settle right in front. Someone whines about it. "You got something to say? I'll cut you," the angry punk replies, all black hair, make up and clothes, "I'll cut you." There is no further argument. It's funny how frightening it was to hear that, considering how willing I'd always been to cut myself.

The rush toward the seats when we are finally let in is terrifying. It's lucky that nobody is killed. If we got seated according to arrival time, we would be front and center, easy, but in the melee, we manage only 8th row. Lesser, but more athletic fans, fare better. It's still pretty great. My mother even winds up buying a ticket and seeing the show from the nosebleed seats. She isn't chaperoning, she goes by herself because she really likes The Cure. My mom is so cute like that. My sister and I hadn't grown up with music in the house. As a matter of fact, my parents aren't aficionados of any kind. No passions, no interests. So, since there is very little in the way of cultural stimuli being presented to us, we find it on our own and give it back to her. Sweet symbiosis.

Mom doesn't like everything that I am listening to, especially as I grow older and my tastes grow harder and darker. Most of my Smiths posters have now been stripped to allow for the large clamped skull of Ministry's "Mind is a Terrible Thing to Taste" poster, and the violent red of the one for Skinny Puppy's "Rabies." My grandmother saw the posters and asked my mother if I was on drugs. Mom told her that I wasn't, and thought she was telling the truth. No one ever asks me that question personally, though. I'm sure I would respond similarly, in content, if not in truthfulness.

We see Skinny Puppy live at the Ritz and it is the most amazing thing I've ever seen. Sure, I am on a little acid, but the theatrics are remarkable enough on their own. A black and gnarled tree revolves on stage with severed limbs hanging from it. The lead singer, Ogre, is wearing a suit laden with blood packs, from which he draws with a syringe, squirting the result onto the front of the crowd. Per usual, that's where I have positioned myself. Ogre's "singing voice" is an anguished, distorted growl. I think he is so hot. After the show Ellen takes a picture of me on her bed, proudly splattered with Ogre's faux fluids.

We aren't all about clubs and music. Sometimes my friends and I do normal kid stuff...sort of. We play Scrabble and drink iced-tea. We have our own amended Scrabble rules in which whoever is winning at the time has to wear this ridiculous umbrella hat that Gina has, and if you have more than two of a letter, you have to lick and stick the third to your forehead. I guess we are a little weird, but we relish it.

We decided to all dress up as dead cheerleaders for Halloween. We even go so far as to ask the actual cheerleaders to borrow their getups. They are into the joke of all of the freak girls being cheerleaders for Halloween, probably because of Nirvana's "Smells Like Teen Spirit" video having reached its populist fever pitch. Of course, the girls don't know that we plan on adding nooses and wrist-slits. Ellen says she is going to affix a bloody Cabbage Patch doll between her legs, peeping out the bottom of the skirt. What a sick-o. I love it.

We have to put the kibosh on the whole scheme when a cheerleader who'd graduated the year prior dies in a car accident. At least there are some boundaries to our bad taste. I kinda think we should still go ahead with it, you know, as long as nobody puts tire tracks on themselves. I have very little in the way of limits.

I start dating Al. We have a great connection. He's much smarter than Jason, but more like a gay best friend. We fool around a little, but it seems like more of an afterthought. It doesn't amount to anything. He even bets me that I can suck his dick and he won't get aroused. You may think this just a young man's ploy to get some head, but nope! Always one to prove a point, I take the challenge and sure enough, can't best him. It's not great for my self-esteem, deriving it, as I do, from the male reaction to me. Al tells me that I can pull off cute, but not sexy. Maybe that is because I am still 15, asshole. When looking for sexy, you should probably avoid little girls. Still, Al does provide me with one of the most romantic moments of my young life when I walk to meet him halfway after he'd taken the train to see me. Why he doesn't have his license at 19, I never ask. But I am sitting on this wood slat fence when I see him come into view. It looks like he is just going to pass me by, doesn't even see me, but instead he swoops over and kisses me, dipping me over the side of the fence. Hot. MMMph. That's how I want my love. Cinematic.

When Jason hears that Al and I are getting together, he suddenly reappears. It has been 6 months or so since our time together and he need only turn in my general direction to beckon me back. We hang out together and he sings along to The Cure's "Boys Don't Cry" for me, using Robert Smith's lyrics to say he wants me back. See, THAT's what I'm talking about! Give me a pretty picture, a dramatic moment. Just like the movies.

THIRTY-NINE

I am still doing plays. I had to stop riding horses because we've run out of money, but I still do the children's shows. Now I have to wear wigs all the time because princesses don't have shaved, pink hair.

I audition for and get a role in a Main Stage show at the theater, an Agatha Christie play called "Spider's Web." I have to be a young English girl, the only juvenile in the cast. It is a blast. I forget, sometimes, to bring a prop on stage with me, but I can cover for that. I'm sure it probably bugs the grownups, but they are nice to me. The younger men in the show, especially, become my buddies. Thom - with an h - who was my teacher that had drafted me into performance there, is in the cast. He almost murders me, but winds up dead himself. In the show, I mean. He is handsome and effete. As he applies his stage make-up one night alone with me in the dressing room, he looks at his own reflection and says, with utmost seriousness, "It is a wonderful thing to know great beauty." He breaks out laughing at himself and I join in. "You will know it too, someday," he tosses over his shoulder at me as he leaves to make his entrance. I am so pleased by this. I hope he is right. I feel so ugly. And it seems nothing is so important in this world as how you look.

After the show tonight, I am going to a party that Mark Lanzer is having. Through parental absence or neglect, he is going to have a keg and everything. It is rumored that he is going to hook up with me tonight, or at least I have convinced myself that he will, but when I get there, he has asked out Lindsay Tannenbaum, that same bitch that had beaten me up so many years ago. She is so fucking bland, so whiney. Well-dressed, though, and a cheerleader now. That's fine, that's fine. I drink. Phil Leach is there and figures, rightly, that I will be a willing participant in whatever salacious activity he has in mind, despite the fact that we haven't spoken since our drainpipe rendezvous. We walk down the block and settle next to a neighbor's house. I tell him that I can't hook up with him, that I am back with Jason. Phil says he will never know, and I say he deserves it. For breaking up with me the first time, I guess. Paul urges me to suck or fuck his alcohol-sodden self and in a moment of clarity, the awkward sordidness of the situation impels me to leave it.

I see Jason the next day. He holds me closely on the couch in my basement and says he loves me, and that he is so glad we are back together. I start crying. I have to tell him, have to, have to. I'd cheated on him. "Did you suck his dick?" he asks, apparently aware of my proclivities. I had, for a little while, anyway. I nod, apologizing. It was a mistake.

Jason just sits there staring straight ahead, his jaw clenched, his eyes cold. I am cross-legged on the floor, dissolving, begging him to talk to me. He won't. I am smoking a cigarette and hold its fiery point to the skin of my forearm. I noiselessly watch as it sinks into the skin, plunging and cauterizing. I go upstairs to clean it off.

That night, Jason comes out with my friends and I to the trail next to the sump at another local high school. Wantagh High School seems to have much cooler people. They like me. Maybe because they don't really know me. Jason barely speaks to me and I cry. I run off down the trail into the woods by myself. I want someone to follow me, reclaim me in dramatic fashion, and shake me to my senses, hold me. Nobody does. I am always performing these scenes in my mind that nobody else has the script for. I sit down for a while and then walk back. Everyone is ignoring me. I don't blame them. I am an asshole. A stupid childish asshole. I just want some pot or something.

I am smoking pretty regularly now. Jason tells his mom

what I've done and then tells me that she said really awful things about me, and wants to punch me in the face. He doesn't see how he can keep going out with me anymore. Yeah, I know, I understand. I call up Al and we resume hanging out, but he tells me right off that he will never again hook up with me. I, again, take this as a challenge, but he bests me on this one as well. Not at Trivial Pursuit though, I totally kick his ass the one night we all try playing that. He thinks he is so smart. He actually is. He doesn't go to college, though, I don't know why. Probably because he is too busy getting high with 15-year-old girls.

One day I walk halfway to the train station to meet him, as was our custom, and attempt to recreate the magical moment we'd once shared. I sit on the top slat of that wooden fence post and blam - it slams to the ground with me on it. I hear Al howling with laughter from his vantage point 50 yards away. It is pretty funny. Humiliating, but I have to admit, funny. And so emblematic of my life.

Without Al to hook up with, I am in need of a suitor. Jason's friend Brent will do nicely. He is really lovely to look at if you ignore his incredibly juvenile tendencies. Or embrace them. Brent can drool down at least three feet and then suck it back up into his mouth. When we first hook up at Hotel Leningrad, I duck underneath him and catch his saliva in my mouth. I am disgusting. But, then, what is kissing, really?

I even take Brent to a family function where he proceeds to ask my cousin if she masturbates, which causes not a little awkwardness. Jealousy on my behalf too, because my cousin is really hot in that bleached blond, blue-eyed, huge tits way, which seems to me the only acceptable way to be hot.

Brent regularly calls me a slut, and when I get angry, he says he is kidding. After going down on him in the woods and hooking up with half his zip code, he has the grounds to say such a thing; I just don't think it's his place. He should thank me, really, seeing as how my slutdom benefits him directly. I tell him not to call me that again and he apologizes in all sincerity, pausing before he adds, "slut." I break up with him right there. He starts crying, which is pretty ridiculous. I think he is faking it. We'd only gone out for three weeks.

I stop dating within that circle of friends, finally, probably because there were no cute ones left. So, I start dating Vince, whom I meet, where else, but at Hotel Leningrad. I had seen him there for weeks and the night we meet I'd promised myself that I am going to talk to the hot Michael Stipe-looking guy. Okay, I know that doesn't sound so alluring. He is like Michael Stipe but sexier. He is yet another nineteen-year-old and shows me a scar on his arm from where he tried to erase himself. With an eraser. I think that is so cool and try it the next day. Smarts pretty bad, erasing your flesh does. Vince also lives in an apartment with his mother who is, yes, a school bus driver, which is a pretty weird coincidence if you ask me. My surprising aptitude for charming parents is lost on her. She doesn't speak to or even look at me. Might as well not get used to me, I guess, it's not likely to last.

This kid is so nuts, he makes me feel well-balanced. I'm arguing with him on the phone when I hear a pause and then a thud. When I ask what the noise was, he says it was his head banging against a counter. Vince has a lying problem too. I certainly seem to have a type. He tells me of getting jumped by six guys and fending off five before the last one sucker punched him. He also shows me the dent in his Zippo where a bullet had struck, saving his life. I smile and nod. Maybe say wow. I don't outwardly question him, I don't care. Maybe these things had happened. It's a crazy world. It doesn't matter. I have a boyfriend. Despite my best efforts, I only ever go down on him. He never reciprocates and we never have sex. I attempt to take him one day near the end of our tenure, on the floor of the laundry room in my basement, with our friends in the next room. He doesn't want to. What the fuck is that about? I break up with him.

His friend Scott tries to take me out, but Scott, at 20, seems somehow too old for me, more so than 19-year-old Vince or Al. He gets me high and drives me around in his converted electric company van, which has, in its caged rear portion, and entire living room set up. He kisses me roughly so that his teeth scrape me, and takes off his shirt, I guess hoping that I will follow suit. No such luck, buddy. I can be pretty reserved sometimes, if I don't like a person. Really quite a prude.

So, I dip back into the Leningrad pool and fish out a bunch of skinheads from Suffolk County. Gina and I take the train out to meet them in a parking lot. They are straightedge, meaning they don't drink or do drugs, so I don't see how I am going to have any fun tonight. At least they aren't into the hatred of other people thing, as are many skins. If they are, they are hiding it. I am glad at least, that no minorities are beaten or disparaged in my presence. I consider myself pretty open-minded for a girl who grew up in an all-white town.

One of the guys, Richey, tries to kiss me. When I say that he tries, I don't mean that I don't reciprocate, but that he fails utterly. Never before have I taken part in anything so lacking in passion or skill. His tongue lolls about in the right-hand corner of his mouth like a stroke victim. I almost throw up all over him. I compromise by not calling him again.

FORTY

You might be wondering about school. You know, that thing at which I used to excel? Well, I'm getting by, which is miraculous because I have my mind on just about everything else. I don't know if it's from the bullying or my mental state, but every minute that I sit in one of those chairs-attached-to-desks, I want to crawl right out of my skin. Jump right out of the window. Go right out of my mind.

I don't know how I bear it. In French class, all I can remember is the translation of "I'm not wearing any underwear." I figure this could get me pretty far, should I find myself in France. It is one of the more fun classes and I still hate it. My head is swimming and I excuse myself to go to the bathroom. Because the French class is in the annex, the closest bathrooms are in the gym, through the locker room. I walk through the row of open lockers, the purses sitting on benches. Just like junior high, nobody locks anything up. I root through the first purse I see, then the second. A master lock sits unengaged on a tall standing locker, and I remove it. Then I remove the cash from the purse inside. I net about $40 in all and return to class. Things are looking up. This pot isn't paying for itself.

I spend all my money on partying. Truly, for a 15-year-old my freedoms are near limitless. We are still at Hotel Leningrad every weekend. Of course, my mom lets me. I am so miserable, and being there and "dancing," it makes me feel better. This is not to say that we aren't dancing, but that it isn't the sole reason for attendance. Gina has got an older friend named Rhoda now. Rhoda has a fancy Dodge Stealth because her father just died. That's what she got. Now released from the prison of parental conveyance, we can really let loose.

Rhoda got some acid, so we drop it when we we're about

five minutes away from the club. My friend Libby that I'd met at horse camp is with us. Her sister is over 21 and bears a striking resemblance, so Libby uses her ID and buys us some vodka. After the Jell-O-barfing incident, you'd think I had learned. We buy Tropicanas and drain them halfway to spike them. See that? Temperance.

The other girls go inside as Rhoda and I walk to the side of the club to nurse our juice-plus. Two guys pull alongside us in a car. "Great," we confer, "here's where we get hit on." They get out of the car and approach us, but love is not their aim. Their car is unmarked, but they are in full police uniforms. They ask us what we are doing. "Going to the club," we say. They ask for our juice boxes and we hand them over, stupidly. They don't technically have a right to smell our juice, but smell it they do. They ask how we got there and Rhoda has the presence of mind to say we'd been dropped off. They get in their car to give us beer tickets, a $50 fine that has to be paid in person, with a parent. As I stand by the driver's window, with the officer scribbling away, his car starts to expand and contract. The acid is kicking in. Right here, right now. It's hysterical. A smile creeps across my face.

FORTY-ONE

So, it's summer. I'm going out with this guy Mike Beale that I met, where else, at Hotel Leningrad. It's getting kind of ridiculous that I procure all my love interests there. He lives a half hour away and my mom gave up on driving me to see men after Jason. Since then it's been reliance on trains and older friends. Fuck that. Dad's Oldsmobile is sitting in front of the house idle while he is in Chicago or Cooperstown or wherever he is off to, selling small pieces of cardboard to other desperate men. The spare keys are readily available. I can drive, sure. I've never tried it before, but how hard can it be? My friends thrill as I pick them up for the adventure. We drive along Sunrise Highway, which was nicknamed "danger highway" by my mother, for its large claim on the lives of drag racers. I meet no danger, however, our trip is uneventful. Even hanging out with Mike is uneventful. He doesn't really do it for me, I am just killing time. He's way too well-adjusted to interest me. His friend Tyler is hotter, but Libby has started dating him. Libby is blonde, pretty. She was the only other girl at horse camp who didn't have her own horse and we bonded over that. She credits me for her introduction to good music. It's nice to be a positive influence in some way. Of course, I'd also given Libby her first hit of acid that night at Hotel Leningrad, but other than that, yeah: positive influence.

I give Mike a first as well. He's a virgin. I hadn't been with anyone but Jason to this point, and I am ready to have sex again. Well, I want to, whether I am ready to or not. I get a ride over to Tyler's, where he and Mike have been drinking by the pool on a sweltering August day. I down a beer, which is enough to intoxicate me. I hadn't brought a bathing suit, but I strip down to my underwear and dance around the pool. Look at me, look at me. Mike takes me inside to Dylan's room.

After an hour and a half, he still hasn't cum. As far as I know, that isn't supposed to happen with virgins. Maybe because he was drinking? Nervous? Who cares? I am bored. I am insulted. We hang out one time after that. His friends and I all get high but he doesn't. Everything he says annoys me. I break up with him. I need to find something to love.

I think I should maybe go back to dancing school. I used to love that. Libby has a place where she goes, so I figure I'll go back with her. Mom takes me to check it out and I get in there and start crying. I guess that last experience really had gotten to me. Hard to tell, I cry about everything. Regardless, I sign up for class. I stand in a line with the girls, all of whom look more like women next to me, who is all scrawny and stretched out. The teacher does a routine for us to follow and the others repeat it flawlessly. I lag behind watching to see what comes next. I can't keep up, I am awkward and confused. I feel like an idiot. Puberty had rendered me all gangly limbs and misfiring synapses. I tell mom that I am just too scarred to continue, that Yasmin has ruined me for dancing. What a travesty! And I had been so gifted! The truth is I just can't do it anymore. Mentally, physically, whatever...I can't do it.

My dancing is different now. I swing my arms and legs in opposition to each other as guitars race and men with distorted voices howl. I careen back-first into the bodies of other teens, each of whom probably feel just like me inside, and each crash is a sweet release. Most of the time it is just guys in the pit, and my boldness and relative femininity is rewarded with free CDS from the DJ. He is on loan from that local new wave station, and thereby a celebrity to me. Tonight, I stare at my options, a choice between two CDS by bands I don't care for at all. I ask if he has anything else. He calls me spoiled. I am so offended, but he is right.

This DJ doesn't even know me, but he busts me. As an

emissary of the station I adore, I respect him, and his reproach is thusly met with a self-conscious sadness instead of my customary bitter bile. "No I'm not," I protest. I feel so underprivileged, laughably enough. I buy all my own clothes from thrift stores...I can't afford horseback riding anymore. This is my home, this club, my safe-place - and the DJ just destroyed me. I grab a CD and leave. It's Straightjacket Fits. Ha. I go back out to dance some more and get slammed across the room, my head striking the metal barrier that surrounds the dance floor. It seems my femininity is no longer being taken into account. The people are out there for blood.

We had to catch a ride home tonight, and my mom isn't going to be at the club to pick us up for a half hour. I am sitting with Gina outside on the stoop when two familiar faces arrive. It's Richey, the skinhead whose kiss I dissed, and his friend Greg. They aren't happy to see me. They have with them two of the most frightening, shaved-headed girls that ever walked the length of Long Island. They surround us as we sit there, small and smoking to occupy ourselves. They yell at me the kind of non-specific slander of those who lack actual opinions. I am a fucking bitch. An asshole. A slut. Okay, maybe that last one is true. Maybe it is all true.

For a girl who comes off as ready to fight at any time, I sure do back down easy. Thoughts of retaliation, of self-defense, are lost in my torrent of tears. I fear saying anything against my tormentors - like, "Hey, you can't just hate me because I didn't like this guy, that's not my fault" - will result in a painful demise via the stomping of 4 pairs of combat boots. My crying raises more ire. I am pathetic, they say, a baby. This is also true. I don't know why I don't invite their slaughter of me, just let them put an end to it all. I am everything they say and worse. They spit on me.

Eventually, they grow tired of my tears and go inside.

The Brink

My mom shows up. I don't tell her what happened, but I tell her that I don't want to go there anymore. I am tired of it.

FORTY-TWO

I am tired of being 15 too. When I turn 16, I can get my permit and get a better job. My father, ignorant of the lessons I had given myself, attempts to teach me how to drive. You can't learn anything from a man with no patience. He snipes at me like he does to other drivers who don't share the road according to his dictate. "Fool," he exclaims at my errors. I throw the car in park and fly back into the house. "He's so awful," I cry to my mother. And she had thought the driving lessons would foster bonding.

I can't stand up to my father, but also can't resist standing up to anyone else who gets in my way (gangs of skinheads notwithstanding.) I hate to see anyone mistreated. A nasty fellow in the mall at Christmas time was haranguing an overwhelmed sales girl about how long he's been waiting. Overhearing the bitter stream with which he drowned her, I stop in my tracks and smile broadly in his direction. "Sir, lighten up, it's the holidays!" I beam. Contrary to how it must sound, I really do have a big bunch of sunshine on reserve within me, but it can easily shift from warm to burn. He looks me up and down, scoffs and shakes his head. Never one to back off a challenge that doesn't actually threaten me, I smile and query, "Sir, why do you look upon me so disdainfully?" I love to throw folks off my slacker scent with faux-Victorianisms and a 50-cent word now and again. He sends knives at me with his eyes, and then his mouth. "Have you looked in the mirror lately?" He's got me there, in my long johns and camouflage, I am not the picture of respectful womanhood. Still my anger boils up within me as I shout at him through the holiday crowd, "I do, every day, and I am beautiful!' He's already walked away.

My mounting bad attitude and poor survey-returns get

me fired from the survey job. I am too sensitive for it anyway. Long Island guys seem to find it funny to get up in your face and shout "NO!" when you ask to survey them. They laugh and high-five each other as another little piece of your soul withers. Finding jobs for anti-social 15-year-olds is not an easy task. I am babysitting poison, and now I look the way I do. I think my boots and partial baldness are adorable, and my mom admits that she does too, but I am less appealing to the standard human.

To wit, I'm hanging outside of the local bowling alley, when two guys roll by and pause as I smoke my cigarette. I am sure they are checking me out. I try to look nonchalant. "You're a mess," they exclaim as they drive away. I scream "fuck you" at their retreating fender. Here I thought they were going to hit on me. I don't know why I always think that.

Thankfully, my dad's friend owns the Hallmark store in the mall and they say they'll hire me as a favor, but I have to do something about my hair. I still have that wig from doing plays, and that's what I wear to cover my "individuality." It is big and biliously brown. Customers must think I have cancer. Poor thing.

Working there is hell, but then, it's hard to separate that feeling from when I'm not working. Being in the aisles means you have to go through making sure no envelopes have been misappropriated, which they always are. Working as a cashier means looking at the back of the card for the last three digits under the bar code. That's the price of the card. You're dealing with customers beset by obligation. They carry with them the angst of attempted communication. They don't want to be there either.

It's really busy in the store today. The line stretches to the back of the store as I tap away at the register, never fast enough. I can't do another card. Can. Not. Do. Another. Card.

Can't see another impatient and uncaring face. I'd had my lunch break only an hour ago. I will be here for three more hours. Three. More. Hours. Three hours of "Hi, how are you doing today? Would you like to join our frequent shopper club, when you buy 10 ca- no? Okay..." Flip the card, key it in, take the money, give the change. "Thanks, and have a great day." Have a great day. I always smile really broadly. I always really mean it. I give them too much of myself. I can't do it anymore. I certainly can't do it for three more hours. I will have nothing left. What can I do? What can I...I start blinking my eyes heavily. I gasp. I send my eyes into the back of my head and fall to the floor. I try to make my wig fall off so that the people will say, "Oh, isn't that terrible? They made that girl wear a wig to cover her hair and the heat of it caused her to faint!" Nobody says that. They leave me there until an ambulance comes. That's pretty smart, I don't think you're supposed to move someone who has fallen. They try to revive me but I am out. I don't know why I pretend to stay out so long. All the less to deal with, I guess. It's a lovely reprieve.

My father is working at his friend's baseball card store nearby and he makes it there pretty quickly, so that he is able to get into the ambulance with me.

The EMT says my name, takes my blood pressure. I flutter my eyes. I am such a good actress. They run tests at the hospital but can't find anything wrong. That's because there isn't anything to find. They put it down to exhaustion and my minimal food intake. I try to blame a wig-derived heat stroke, but am denied. I tell dad on the way home that I'd just faked it so I could get out of there. "No way," he says. I was out when he got there, he says. Out cold. I insist, but he refuses to believe me. Not only does he always lie, but he's willing to support my untruths. Okay, fine. But I don't want to go back to that job again.

FORTY-THREE

Eleventh grade is going to be better. I am looking forward to another season of doing children's theater. It has been two years, and I've had my picture in the paper about a dozen times, which nobody in school ever acknowledges or congratulates me on. No matter, it makes me feel good regardless. Last year, after a show, a man came down the line where we stood greeting children as they exited. He leaned into me with his finger in my face. "You're gonna make it," he said to me. I don't know what power he had to make such proclamations, but I believed him, and it gave me hope.

Last season, the director Ken had told me the first show in the fall would be "Little Red Riding Hood," and that I would be Little Red. The call doesn't come. I wonder what's happening. I should've heard something by now. I call the theater. Bart, who works in the office, is my buddy. He has a band called "Francis Farmer, My Hero," and their only album traces the life of the obscure, deranged actress. I have to admire that, even if the music is not my cup of English Breakfast. We talk about music and movies. He loves the movie "Heathers" too and calls me Winona, which thrills me to no end. He thinks I am a neat kid. I need that. People I admire validating me. Anyone validating me. I can tell it is hard for him to tell me that they have started rehearsals, and that they had cast all new folks. It was decided the theater needed some new blood. New blood. Right. I swallow hard. I deal with it. Progress, maybe?

I get a call from Ken less than a week before they are supposed to open. Little Red has been a "problem." Can I come into rehearsal the next day? Can I learn the script in five days? Of course I can. I am a pro. He says he'll call me back with the rehearsal time. I am going to show them. I relish the opportunity to save the day. Talk about validation! I can't wait...but wait I do.

It's 5 o'clock the next day. I imagine we'd probably be starting in an hour or two. I call the theater again and get Ken this time. He is quiet. They'd worked things out with Little Red Whining Prude, and they are going to go forward with her. It's too late to change things now. Right. "I wish you'd told me," I say coldly. I hang up.

For someone who once promised to off herself the moment her stream of performance came to an end, I handle it well. Maybe because I still have acting possibilities to look forward to. The year prior, I'd auditioned for the BOCES Cultural Arts Center. Normally, BOCES programs are trade school-type training grounds for delinquents and those with no hopes for future education. I don't know what the acronym stands for...maybe "bordering-on-cretin education series." The Cultural Arts Center though - on the opulent north shore of Long Island - was for us creative types, with tracks for music, dance, art and acting. I got in but then, I don't know if there was anyone who didn't. Some schools allow their students to attend the full day there, but for our cheap ass school it was just a half-day thing. This is still a vast improvement. I deem BOCES my forthcoming savior.

Although there are a bunch more for dance, I am one of three girls from my school attending the acting program. Marissa Scorcese is one of them, she had once been to my house in elementary school. We called a talent agent whom we found in the yellow pages - attempting discovery - though neither of our mothers would take us to see her so we - I - wrote a poem bemoaning our sad fates. Marissa's last name is an unfortunate coincidence that renders her connectionless. Abby Bennett is the other girl, the one from the "Cats" screaming match and the bad kiddie-goth band. The three of us don't talk much anymore, ensconced as I usually am in my safety-blanket of

Walkman music for the half-hour ride each way. They are both pretty normal. The thing about being a freak in high school is you feel superior to those who once ostracized you. It gets you by, I guess. You find comfort only in your own kind.

Therefore, my glee is likely evident, and possibly frightening, as I spot the fiery-headed girl at the buses after that first day of class. "Is that rubine?" I ask her, referring to the color of Manic Panic. "No…" she says as she looks at me uneasily, "…flamingo pink." I take off my hood to reveal the rubine stripes I'd added the night before in a twisted sort of back-to-school ritual. I could see her accept me right away, sisters of pigment as we are.

Her name is Eryn. She is a painter. She makes figure studies in oil, twisting their forms into the grotesque. We become fast friends, sharing as we do that great glue of unity, marijuana. We sneak behind the school's ventilation system daily to get high before the long ride back to our respective schools. She is from Baldwin, near my grandparents. Once I have my permit, my mom lets me drive to Eryn's house. Legally, a permit is supposed to be used for going to work or school, but my mom is just glad I have a new friend. So am I. Gina has been hanging out with Rhoda more and more. I can tell that I'm an annoyance to them.

The school is okay too. I mean, just okay. I only like one teacher, the one for straight acting. The musical theater teacher is a bitch, and she is married to the movement teacher, who is an asshole. He had been in the film versions of "West Side Story" and "Saturday Night Fever" and has clearly never gotten over his successes despite the silly, stunted suburban training ground it has landed him in. I think most of the other students are hacks, which doesn't seem to prevent them from getting preferential treatment. It always feels like everyone else is being so acclaimed while a more heavily scrutinizing eye lays on me.

The accompanist asks if I smoke. He says he can hear it when I sing. He asks why I don't train my voice more and I tell him that I am not interested in musical theater. Anymore. Even in regular high school, I refuse to go out for the musical theater shows, seeming as they did to me now, to be lame. I'd gone out for "You Can't Take it With You" when I was a freshman, and although the other competitors commended my audition for the awkward ballerina girl, the role was given to a graduating cheerleader who was a really good dancer. Being a good dancer is SO not the point of that role, but I had to bow to the seniority thing. 10th grade was too intense for me to audition...I don't even know what play they did, but I am finally given a part in 11th grade, in that other high-school theater classic, "The Man Who Came to Dinner." Appropriately, I am the crazy old aunt who lives in the attic and appears only occasionally to great comedic effect. I consider doing the performance on acid, but thankfully give up that notion. I never even get high for a show or rehearsal. I always take that stuff very seriously. Well, on the last night the lead guy and I do this riff thing where he falls out of his wheelchair and hearkens to that great line of advertising past, "I've fallen and I can't get up." Then when he does get up and back into his chair, I herald it as a miracle. Comedy magic, I'm telling you.

There is a party on the beach after the closing show. I go there with the gray from the play still in my hair. Mark Lanzer is there. As he sits next to me around the bonfire, my heart thrills. We talk about my combat boots, and I am too drunk to tell if he is making fun of me. I declare my Docs to be fire resistant. "Look!" I exclaim. I put my leg into the flames.

I feel the searing of white-hot metal into the back of my calf with an imagined hiss of burning flesh. I pull it out. "Ouch," I whimper. "I think that hurt." Praise be to alcohol's numbing effects in that moment, if not to its dumbing effects that caused the idiocy in the first place. Two parallel, three-inch long lines, from the metal canister in which the fire is contained, had singed into my leg right above the top of my boots. I am right, though, my boots are fine.

After we leave the beach, Rhoda is going to take us to a club called E. I don't even know yet that E is a drug, but I am going to the club nonetheless. We all get 40 ounces of the inappropriately-named malt liquor Crazy Horse and chug them in Rhoda's Stealth before we go inside. E is a cinder block with neon lights. The music throbs as we stumble in the darkness. After not so long, we are all passed out and vomiting in different areas of the club. I lay on a dubious sofa, puking over the side. Gina sits in a chair puking on herself while being hit on, a fact that really impresses me. When my head is finally somewhat clear, I realize that it's 2am and I should be home. I rouse Gina, whose suitor is no doubt disappointed at the revocation of his easy mark. We can't find Rhoda, though. We look everywhere until finally landing in the bathroom where she is on the floor of one of the stalls. "Get up," we tell her, "you have to drive us home."

We stop for gas along the way and Rhoda's car dives over the median. Gas attendants should really report things like that. It is incredible fortune that we arrive home in one piece. It's funny to be grateful to be alive when you so frequently wish yourself dead.

When I return to school on Monday, I learn of the two tragedies. Gianni Giancoli, he of the kindergarten beatings, had flown off the back of a motorcycle and died. In high school life he'd been a giant, a football player rumored to fuck girls in bathrooms as early as 7th grade. We'd resolved our differences and he was now one of the few people who would be nice to me. He would compliment my hair, sprayed up in a ponytail on my head to let the shaving show. I viewed his praise with skepticism, but it seemed to be delivered in earnest. I don't see how I can go to the funeral, knowing my presence will be questioned and scorned. I feel badly.

That same weekend, a cheerleader's younger brother was killed riding his bike along a busy road. He was only 12. Everyone is walking around the school in a daze, and me with these two scars across my calf, feel somehow responsible, like I'd received physical portents of the impending deaths of those who had wronged me. Sure, the cheerleader's brother is a reach and it's a heady, deluded mindset but then, what can be expected from a girl doing as much acid as I am now?

Acid has become an almost weekly thing, and Eryn and I have become inseparable. We leave behind the kiddie-clubland of Hotel Leningrad and graduate to Manhattan goth clubs. For my 16th birthday, my mom drives my friends and I to the famed club Limelight and picks us up there at 2am. It's a 45-minute drive, at best. Does she go all the way home in between? What does she *do*? I never ask. It never crosses my mind.

Always on my mind, however, is the prospect of meeting a funky metropolitan gentleman to love me. I do meet a promoter for the club who tries to get me a job dancing in the cage there, but that falls through when it's discovered I am not even old enough to officially enter the club. You could be let in those doors if you were to write on a piece of paper that you were of age. That's essentially what I was doing.

When our school decided in 10th grade to start using ID's, they handed out small pieces of paper for us to fill in our name, date of birth and grade. The black-light bulb went off in my head. Who was checking these? Was anyone? Probably not. I wrote that I had been born in 1973 instead of 1976. I made the 0 in my 10th grade look *maybe* like a two. This rendered me 19 in my senior year. The administration collected our slips, and handed them back the next week, laminated.

The fact that my ID rendered me some sort of idiot does not prevent our entrance, nor does it prevent the bartenders from serving us amaretto sours and mudslides and other drinks-of-choice for the 16-year-old set. Drinking is expensive though, as is the Limelight's cover charge, so acid at The Bank becomes de rigueur.

The Bank is, appropriately, a club converted from an old bank. Every week, kids with white faces and black clothes line up for admittance. Eryn and I always drop our hits on the train ride in, and smoke some weed to get things started. Tonight, I am so fucked up by the time I get inside that I place my hand in the outstretched palm of the lace-clad girl at the door. I think it is a very dramatic greeting...turns out she just wants the $5 entry fee.

We all fancy ourselves immortals, and swirl around the dance floor to the droning voices and minor chords, our hands entwined and stretching up artfully in the lights. A man in a black fedora with eye make-up approaches me, wanting to dance. I humor him for a while until he swoons in too close. I go to get a drink. There he is again, ridiculous in his tilted hat. He attempts discourse which I dispatch with the kind of flip and articulate response that I am capable of only with members of the opposite sex who hold no interest for me.

Shadow Project is playing. They are comprised of former Christian Death members and I am a big fan, although even I have to acknowledge that the first track on the CD, which opens with the repeated howl of "death, death, DEATH!" is a little over-the-top.

The spindly and pained-looking players yelp through their heavily orchestrated set. I am transfixed. The lights entrance me. The song is in a loop. It keeps going and going and going and going. I start to get scared. It is stuck. It is never going to end. Eryn and her boyfriend Glen are arguing behind me. I hear my name. I'm not going to look. It keeps going, the music, the arguing. I am trapped in time. This will go on forever. This is hell.

I breathe deeply. "As soon as the song is over, I'll know everything is okay," I think to myself. It continues until it finally crashes to an awkward close. Anticipation hangs in the air. I stare forward and Eryn taps me on the shoulder. I wheel around to see her and Glen staring at me, all pupils and intensity. "Jaime, what are we doing now?" she pleads. I don't know what she means, I don't know why she is asking me. It's like I am the one in control, but I don't want to be.

We settle on the universal answer and retreat to the basement, where it is easy to smoke weed openly without concerns of interference. Suddenly the fedora man is there too and asks to join us. Sure he can. We don't hoard. We're not snobs. Eryn and Glen start dancing and leave fedora man and I to a conversation, which quickly twists in our chemical minds. I start to rifle through my bag.

"What are you looking for?" he asks me.

"I don't know."

"Do any of us?"

"Yes, I think some do."

"Do you?"

"I do."

"I thought you said you didn't."

"Not in that context."

"What context do you mean?"

"A larger one."

"I can take you places."

"I can go myself."

"You think so?"

"I do."

"You think you have more power than me?"

He actually asks that. What's more is, I actually answer. "Yes," I say. We rise, eye to eye from our seated position. We stare into one another's eyes, daring. I don't know what I am supposed to do. I am filled with violence. I do have more power. I know if I swing at him right now, he will drop. I can take him.

Though I'd never done something like that before, never hit a person, I bring back my fist with all the strength I can muster and swing it at his face. I feel no impact. He doesn't fall. He grabs me by my shoulders and throws me on the ground. He lifts my head and slams it back down to the floor. He has more power than me.

I come to on the side of the dance floor with Eryn holding my head and saying my name. We look up to see Glen and fedora man circling each other menacingly on the concrete basement dance floor. The music drones on. The lights flash. Mr. Fedora dashes to the stairs, up and out. Glen follows him but comes back quickly, defeated, as I had been. Fedora man had brandished a knife, apparently, and Glen relinquished his pursuit.

What had happened, they wanted to know. I'm not sure. It was a weird thing. An acid thing. But I had lost. I wasn't supposed to hit him. I lost. We leave, and don't ever go to The Bank again.

The next day is Thanksgiving. I miss it entirely. That is generally my dad's job, bowing out of family functions, but I am following in his footsteps. Even when I do attend, I go and lay down for hours, exhausted by the effort. But Thanksgiving...I don't want to go see my family. Smile and say that everything is great. Be grateful? I don't even want to move.

Mom tells me that my cousin Gayle is very disappointed.

Jaime Andrews

She'd come down with her parents from her home near Boston. I only see her once a year. She is nine and really looks up to me. Well, she looks up to the girl I used to be. I am woken from a pot-fueled nap to my mom telling me Gayle is on the phone. I groggily answer. She has some questions for me. Terrifying. She is supposed to do a report on someone she admires. She picked me. My heart falls. She asks me about doing local theater, about the honor roll, about horseback riding, French horn and being school president. My answers are curt, honest: I don't do those things anymore. I tell her that I like music. I like going out dancing. I leave out the drug part.

FORTY-FOUR

But where am I to go for my hedonistic exploits now? Hotel Leningrad, Limelight, The Bank...they all seem so dark and unpleasant. There are other things going on now. Raves. Same music that they played at that club E that we went to. It was not such a far cry from the industrial music I enjoyed. Meat Beat Manifesto was a bridge between the two. I crossed it.

Rhoda's boyfriend Rob is a rave promoter and there is one coming up next weekend. We don't know where, you never know where. We are told to drive to an intersection and, when we get there, a guy with a flashlight gives us the address of a warehouse a few blocks away. We enter the non-descript building, which swirls with lights and pulses with bass inside. In the corner is a DJ intent on the two turntables before him. The music warps and piques your mind, expanding it. Of course, I am also on two hits of acid.

I inhale deeply as I see someone I know and am not glad to see. It's Greg, the skinhead who threatened to kick my ass outside of Leningrad less than a year before. His hair is a little grown in, athletic shoes have replaced his combat boots, and he wears an oversized, brightly colored t-shirt. He sees me too, and comes over to give me a hug. A hug! Raves had turned this angry man into a fountain of love! Raves are awesome! We all dance and dance and dance and dance and dance. No longer am I thrashing about angrily, but instead moving my body like water in the sea of music.

We go into the city for parties too. The big thing going on is NASA, at The Shelter. It is the progenitor. Old school shit. We aren't regulars. Hell, I'd even say we are posers, but everyone has to start somewhere. The scene is only maybe a year old.

We go, a whole group of us. With us is this scrawny

graffiti writer kid, Connor, a delinquent skater from school, who is one year my junior. As we get into the subway station to go home, his body tenses and he looks around nervously. He doesn't want to get on the train. He doesn't want to come with us. We tell him to calm down, we tell him he is fine. That doesn't help. He doesn't believe us, we are against him. His hands are balled into white-tight fists. His jaw is tensed, his eyes are wild. "I'm gonna die," he yells. "I'm gonna die!" He looks down the subway tunnel. We hold him back in case he is planning on making his proclamation a fact. He struggles free. He just keeps yelling until finally a police officer approaches us.

"Is everything all right?" he asks. We say it is, but Connor, he says "no." No it isn't. He needs help. "No Connor, come on, it's going to be fine, let's go." He doesn't want to come with us. The officer represents safety, and Connor prefers his company to ours. The officer takes him away. "Oh Jesus, he is screwed," we muse en masse. What a stupid choice. We don't see Connor for a while after that, he is grounded for life or something. Joined the Hari Krishna's, I don't know. I don't seek him out or anything.

Apparently in the bathroom of the club, he had sat on the floor in a puddle resulting from a broken vial of liquid acid. I had taken it voluntarily, and am not sure if that really happened to him or if that is the story he concocted to explain to his parents what occurred…I didn't care what the truth was. It was a pretty funny story, though.

I am dating another graffiti guy. He writes "Fact." Yeah, he thinks so. Ron is not up to my usual physical standards, but I am drawn to him nonetheless. He is shorter than me with a belly. He has sunken eyes, a big nose and almost no lips to speak of. Fucking funny guy though, and there is something about him. He always has weed, which could be part of it. He treats me nicely. Once, when I was mad at him, he brought me a rose and went to the mall to douse himself with a sample of Eternity, still my favorite scent of lovers past. He probably stole the rose off a grave or something. Whatever, it is more effort than I have ever seen made on my behalf. Ron tells me he did a big spray-painted mural of my name. I ask him to go see it and he says it was buffed the next day. Another liar.

I don't believe him for a second, but still, it is the thought that counts. Ron really puts the ass in badass. Every time he comes to my house, the whipped cream canisters no longer spray their stuff on my blueberries anymore. Fucker is doing whippits off the nitrous in the cans, I come to realize. He has a slow drawl from growing up in Kentucky and he'll kick your ass if you so much as look at him sideways. My mom hates him. Calls him rat boy. Everyone else calls him Kentucky Fried Ron.

Because he is a skater, and we hang out with a large group of them, it was inevitable that other Long Island skaters would join the congregation. Thusly it isn't long before the skating specters of my past join in the jumping of my neighborhood curbs.

First is Vince. He doesn't talk to or look at me as though I've done something horrible to him. I'm sure in his revisionist history, I had. Even though he is in my town with my friends, I'm certain that my presence is indicative of stalking in his eyes. I just angrily try to stay out of his way. When he starts dating Rhoda, I keep my warnings to a minimum so that they won't be misconstrued as jealousy. I wish her luck, that is all. It takes her less than a month to realize just how far out of his mind he is and she dispatches of him. In a bid for pity, he calls Rhoda to tell her he's been diagnosed with cancer. In his jaw. He is going to have to get chemotherapy. The kind where you don't lose your hair. Jesus, man, if you're going to pull the cancer lie, at least be willing to shave your head. I don't blame him for not wanting to do so, his hair is one of his finer points. Fortunately,

Vince is pretty widely reviled after this move, so I don't have to deal with him anymore.

As if I cannot be spared the presence of lovers past, Jason is the next to join the pack. He starts dating my friend Nora. Not a close friend, a school friend. She is pale with blue, blue eyes and dyed black hair. A pretty piece of trash. I stop talking to her. I would bash her face in but I totally think she could take me.

The first time Jason comes with her to the parking lot we hang out in, I act all happy to see them, and then get on top of his crappy old car and start jumping up and down. He just sits inside and scowls. I am just kidding around, it is funny. We start calling Nora "pork, the other white meat" and I hope aloud that she will have fun picking all his body hairs off of her. They don't last long. Everyone made it pretty obvious that she had tread on sacred ground. Or at least I did.

Jason and Ron wind up becoming friends, naturally. They can tell fantastical stories to one another. Ron tells me that Jason clued him in on a tale of this Asian girl in the city who had been a virgin but would only have sex with him. I snort. "Does he know we slept together?" I ask. Until Ron, Jason thought he'd been my one and only. I'd hooked up with all his friends, yes, but slept with none of them. "Yeah," Ron admits, "he actually told me that story right after I told him."

Ha. I knew it. What a fucking liar.

I had talked to Jason a few times, here and there. It turns out he goes to raves now too. According to him, he practically runs the damn things. Of course, everything in Jason's life is pretty exciting, according to him.

See, he's been working with the Irish mafia and has a new girlfriend, with whom he has united the Irish and Chinese mafias, something that hasn't been done in *years*. He'd always had a thing for Asian women. It was one of the myriad things that threatened me about him. How can anyone ever really love you if you are not their ideal? I congratulate him in all his ridiculousness.

By the next time we speak, he's left the mob because it got too dangerous. A bullet had grazed his head, apparently. Sure, Jason.

None of this stops me from wanting to be with him, for some reason. Nostalgia? I resent him as much as I long for him. Eryn and I invite him to come over with his friend. We all get high and I play with the camcorder that I'd begged for and received for my "sweet" 16. The thinking was that, with my interest in acting, it was an investment. I am going to make movies or something. Mostly, I just film my friends and I when we are high.

Jason sits on the floor playing video games as we roll tape on the couch behind him. I zoom in close on the hair creeping out of the back of his shirt. I pan over to Eryn who whispers, "Is it really worth it?" She takes the camera as I nod emphatically in response, approximating with my hands the size of his manhood. That's me! Sixteen and already such a classy woman of the world.

Jaime Andrews

FORTY-FIVE

I'm filming mom driving me over to Eryn's on New Year's Eve. We are just going to go to a local party she knows about, nothing fancy. As we drive, I put Ministry on her car stereo. The plan was to make a tape of us to send to my sister.

"Mom lip-syncs Ministry while driving down Sunrise Highway - for you Carrie!" is my introduction as I turn the camera on my adorable little mommy, who nods her prim and proper head to the racing first beats of their song "Stigmata." With the opening scream, Mom opens her mouth with as much menace as she can muster. It's not much. My laughter erupts from the passenger seat.

When we get to the party, Kiera, the purple-haired chick who almost attacked me at the hospital is there, by chance. I can see her almost make the choice to still hate me as I approach her. "Hey," I say, trying to be conciliatory, "let's make this year better than the last one, eh?" It's almost nice. I'm not going to send my sister the later part of the tape, where we give a stoned reprisal of the night's events, including an incident where I set fire to the shoelaces of this loud, obnoxious guy. A shame we didn't tape that, really.

I do kinda want to include some footage of when Eryn's friend Tom mimed screwing this stuffed bear to great effect, but then I realize it had been Carrie's bear and she might not appreciate it as much. Instead, I pull apart the leaves of the dining room table, putting my head in the opening and the tablecloth around my neck to give the impression that my severed head is sitting on the table. From this position, I deliver to my sister a monologue - with a British accent, for some reason - telling her that I've been decapitated by the subway doors in Manhattan. I tell my sister that mom must have been right about me going to the city being a bad thing, because now

I am just a head, capable only of rolling around.

In a way, I am separated from my body. With this mixture of the self-loathing I'd received from constant mockery and pride for what I believe looks good. I walk around high school wearing thigh-high stockings and garters with cut off army shorts and a "Clockwork Orange" t-shirt. My social studies teacher says he's pretty sure that such an ensemble is not allowed. Nobody stops me, though, just like nobody stops me from watching "Clockwork Orange" every night before I go to sleep.

By this point, I have earned a sort of begrudging respect in my school. No longer a simpering wastrel, I have become one not to fuck with. Plus, they want my stuff.

It's the grunge revolution, see, so the combat boots they made fun of the year before, they now want to borrow. It is just like in 8th grade when I wore one of those surfer "Bajas" and everyone called me Pancho Villa. The next year, everyone had them and no one bothered to acknowledge my fashion prescience. But now it was, can I borrow your Docs? Can I borrow a band shirt? Farrah, whose open distaste for me has remained since our junior high friendship-by-proxy, actually sent someone to ask me if she could borrow a Red Hot Chili Peppers or Cure shirt for the Jane's Addiction show. Everyone in my school is going to that show. Screw that, it's at Madison Square Garden, not even a small club. In a protest that will make no difference, I decide that I am not going. Further, I send word back to Farrah that one of my shirts wouldn't fit her. She was a bigger girl. What reason do I have to be delicate? When have they ever been delicate with me?

Anyone who dares mess with me feels the wrath. When some younger tough guy on my bus calls me a dyke, I unleash my fury. Awfully defensive, I know. But, see, just the day before, Ron had come by and we'd had sex a total of eight times.

To completion each time, too. Well, his completion, anyway. The slur fills me with rage and I rear back with my portable tape player and strike him in the head, hard. He holds his head and mutters, "crazy bitch," as I scream that I'd had more sex the day before then he ever would in his whole life. An unlikely assessment, but he shuts up. It's a pretty light tape player, the child's one I'd gotten for the hospital, which I continue to brandish with pride. The Walkman doesn't quite do it anymore, I want everyone to hear the twisted shit I listen to. To hear what is going on in my mind.

I don't get in trouble for my attack. I never get in trouble. My mom goes through my bag and finds my pipes and pot and throws them out. Never says anything, just gets rid of them. It's really an annoyance and a waste of money, because I am only going to go buy more.

After my parents go to bed, I always creep out into the backyard to polish off a bedtime bowl. One night, I come back inside to find them in the kitchen. Busted. "What were you doing out there?", my mom asks. Without blinking I tell her that I'd had to fart really bad, and didn't want to smell up the house. Genius. Mom says they thought it smelled like marijuana. "Maybe it's my fart," I say with utmost sincerity. They don't argue. They can't argue.

They don't know what to do with me, poor things. It is decided that I will spend a week with my sister, who is living in San Francisco now. It really is a great idea because, when a young girl is out of control, one should always send her to hang out with a bunch of punks in their early twenties with absolutely no adult supervision.

Carrie lives with 4 other people in an awesome apartment a few blocks off Haight Street. There is a hippie couple that stays mostly in their room, a hot goth-y girl that has a fishbowl of condoms in her room and Brandon. Brandon is right up my alley. 6'5" with dyed black hair and light brown eyes. He is 23. I will have him, oh, I will have him. I decide this when he first presents himself in the kitchen. He jumps in where we are all making breakfast, and strikes a kung-fu pose. When he leaves without eating, the roommates query the origin of his good spirits. "Chrissy must be in town," they say. Damn, I think. He's got a girlfriend.

The whole week is awesome. We go to all these parties and bars. Carrie doesn't mind if I drink, and doesn't say anything when I start smoking weed with Brandon. Everyone has gone to bed and we get high and watch a movie. I don't even know what it is, that's not what's on my mind. I snuggle in close. He is a goner. We retreat to his room and rapturously love until he realizes he doesn't have any condoms. I point out Ilsa's big bowl of them and he is tentative, not wanting to send up a flare that he is about to fuck his roommate's little sister, but good sense prevails and he makes his way down the hall to go fishing.

When he comes back, he introduces me to Chrissy. It isn't a girl at all! No...it's crystal meth. It's really popular in San Francisco right now. I've never heard of it and I've never snorted anything but am certainly not against it. We each take a little and then screw like crazy to thumping industrial music. He has to go to work the next day, but he even leaves a little bit for me by the bed to get me going the next morning. What a sweetie.

I am supposed to meet my sister at the movie theater she works at. Her two years at UCONN and two years at Berkeley have brought her to much the same place I am in life at 16, since I've also started working at a movie theater back home. She has a boyfriend with long dreads and a drinking problem. She doesn't want a "real" job because that isn't very punk rock. The thing about anti-establishment types taking jobs that are beneath them is that you wind up becoming a lowly cog in the machine that you are fighting against. It's no kind of revolt not to use your brain.

But my brain, now, is buzzing. I charge happily uphill to the theater and twitch my way through the film I watch while she works. We walk home together wordlessly. Tonight, we are supposed to have dinner with her biological father and his new wife. We have a few hours to kill, though. I am just going to lay down for a little while...with Brandon.

We smoke a bunch of weed to ease us off the crystal high. We screw and then smoke some more. I am comatose, practically drooling. There is a knock on the door. My sister opens it and asks if I am ready to go. "Go where?" I ask incredulously. "To dinner," she reminds me, with her dad.

When she turned 18, Carrie's dad had contacted her for the first time in almost as many years. He sent her a $100 Bloomingdale's gift certificate for her birthday, a pretty good deal for him if you consider the cost of fatherhood over the 18 years for which he was not liable. He lives in Northern California, so when she went up to Berkeley, they forged some sort of relationship. She has a little half-sister, only four. Carrie's dad is a bartender and still given to the proclivities that forced mom from him so long ago. I guess she made the right decision, or something. Clearly it was a good thing that she married my dad, or I would never have been born. And that is a good thing. Right?

I look up at Carrie with bleary eyes. I can't. I just can't. I am wrecked. I feel really bad, but Brandon consoles me.

When I get back to New York, Ron has hickies from a drunken hookup with some skater whore. I laugh at him and hold his gaze steadily. "That's fine," I say. "You had her, I had Brandon." He asks who Brandon is all the time. It's funny. I am so detached that I've become the ultimate girlfriend. I don't care about a thing. Not to mention, Ron takes glory in telling his fellow skaters that I'd fucked him dizzy in the corner of the parking lot where they all skated. I am proud too. When your sources are limited, you derive pride from wherever you can.

I ask around at school if anyone knows where to get crystal meth. It's a good thing nobody does.

I have my run of this school. The nurse has orders to send me home if I so much as enter her office. I sit in front of the school smoking bowls with the windows of the administrative offices behind me. Every now and again, I dip into the Bank of the Locker Room. No safety precautions are ever taken, no guards or cameras added. No memos about keeping your stuff locked up because of a thief at large. I am just allowed to have my way.

Nobody is safe, either. I ask my friend Kelly if I can get some weed from her. She says sure, she has gym next and will meet me afterwards. Ding! Now, Kelly isn't a *friend* friend. We talk. She is spacey and walks around as a sort of Janis Joplin shadow in scarves and boots. We don't hang out or anything. So, it's not so big a deal that during the next period, I ask for my standard bathroom pass and aim for the big, fringed leather target in which resides my prize.

When I see her shortly thereafter, I brandish a $5. I just want a joint, after all. She is crestfallen… apparently, her pot has been stolen! I sympathize, and yet show disappointment at my fizzled connection. It is a marvelous performance.

Despite this obviously profound talent, I am not having as easy a time in my acting school. You'd think I would go in for that sort of thing, but it just isn't right. Or I'm not. I've had so much fun in acting classes before, but this seems like a bastardization of performance, executed by the untalented. Okay, really just that "West Side Story" guy's wife. Lynn. I assume she was hired as part of some sort of package deal.

The tension between us mounts over the year. She knows my efforts are half-assed, but even still, I believe them to be more deserving of the praise she heaps upon my other, more traditionally attired classmates. She gives no helpful feedback to anyone. She watches, judges and tells stories of her husband's crusty old successes. She disgusts me.

Her husband is gross too. He is clearly still basking in the light cast by his former glory. He teaches our dance class. I don't care about dance anymore. I don't want to do it at all, even. It makes me angry, it overwhelms me.

Today, I particularly don't want to be here, nor do I wish to proceed with the entirety of my day, so I pull my fainting bit. Go to the hospital and everything. Eryn tells me later that when she saw the paramedics rush by her studio, she knew it was for me.

Eryn is my best friend now. Gina has gotten closer to Rhoda and doesn't have much use for me anymore. So, every day, Eryn and I get high after classes, and on Fridays when we have movement class together, we get high beforehand and laugh hysterically as we exaggerate the moves we have to perform. I usually don't even take the bus back to school now, Eryn drives me because it's on the way back to her school. We get totally wrecked and I'm able to get through the day. I'm pretty sure that I do better than I would if I were sober. While high, I take an essay test on "The Scarlet Letter" and score a 98, even though I didn't read most of the book. I guess that I know from disgraced women.

That's partially what brings Eryn and I together. We're the outcasts, the ones that other girls snicker about as they pass them in the halls. I mean, let's be real: even amongst the outcasts in my school, I am an outcast. Now Eryn feels like the best friend I've ever had. We understand each other, both suffering, as we do, from mental monsters. We're both artists, we create, we suffer, we party, we repeat.

Eryn and I go to this elaborate local playground all the time to smoke our weed and play. We swing as high as we are, and, once at the apex, we jump from our seats and fly. We hide from each other in the maze of wooden structures and go down the slides backwards. Where are all the children?

We go to see concerts that I don't remember. We do acid at Pigface. Early on, someone hands us a slip of paper that says "Sophia Run, sheep bah, what do you do?" The entirety of the show – which I'd been really excited about – becomes a mental mission to crack this riddle. We see Einsturzende Neubaten and get super-duper high. I love the opening act, but pass out on the floor immediately following it, waking only to hear the final, deafening crash of metal which closes the show of this arguably very loud band, which I have somehow just managed to sleep through.

Our friendship is fecund with inside jokes and shared amusements. To her, I am the Empress of China Birds. She, in turn, is Cleopatra the Nile Bitch. We are Frik and Frak and fuck you, you liar. We never stop quoting this Howard Stern tape of Giuliani and Dinkins debating for the NYC mayoral seat. It's really funny. You'll just have to trust me. Though I'm not sure why anyone would do that.

FORTY-SIX

I proceed to clear the excess, the annoyance from my life. I break up with Ron, claiming he can do no more than fight and write. It had gotten boring, so I dispatched of him poetically. The only thing that I have to show for our relationship is a black Acme skate hat that he'd given me. It looks pretty badass on me. I love that fucking hat. Of course, I wind up leaving it at some kid's house party when I'm wasted. I think I had taken it off so we could fool around. Out of boredom, more than anything.

In school, my amazingly maintained accelerated status means that I have Chemistry this year. The teacher's droning delivery drills into my brain until I can stand it no more. He repeats everything in threes, pausing as though to allow the class to interject the answer. Nobody ever does. It so maddens me that by the time he tells us that deci- is....ten, deci- is.....ten, deci- is....I shout, "TEN!!!" really loud and storm out of the room. What a fucking waste of time. I drop the class. I don't need it to graduate. Screw that. Under other circumstances, I probably would have liked Chemistry too...I certainly seem to like chemicals.

I drop honors social studies too. The teacher, Mr. Chasen, is so smug and condescending. I hate that. Even though I am pulling a just-below-100 average, the disdain with which he handles other students after they proffer wrong answers infuriates me. It's just not a very supportive learning environment. Once, when he had crushed the hopes of a girl who incorrectly guessed the reasons for the Magna Carta or something, I said out loud, "She tried." That's me: defender of the weak, voice box of the disenfranchised. Mr. Chasen and I have daily wars with our eyes and wrestling matches with our words. Even the fact that Mark Lanzer is in this class can't keep me here. When I stalk in for Mr. Chasen to sign the transfer memo, Mark asks me where I am going. I reply, right there before the class, as I stand by Mr. Chasen's side, that I had told the principal that if I didn't get transferred away from this teacher immediately that it was possible I would kill him. I'm not arrested or anything. I told you, I run this school.

I am, however, suspended with some frequency. As the bell rings, I walk into a class that has a substitute and laugh as he tells me to get a late pass. "Oh my god, I'm going to hit you!" I say, non-threateningly. Bing! Suspension, for threatening a teacher. Come on! It is just a figure of speech. I can't always blame the administration though. Clearly there is a pattern at work. I even get suspended from the acting school.

After class, Eryn and I sit behind the school, with our ritual joint, in her old Chevy. Through our laughter and the smoke, we don't realize that there is someone walking toward us until they are 10 feet away. It's an adult. We watch, transfixed in horror, as he walks up to Eryn's window and knocks on it. She rolls it down, letting out a billow of fragrant air. "I don't know what to do about this," is all he says. Then he turns around and walks back into the school. Oooookaaaay. We laugh, what the hell was that about? We drive away, relieved at our crisis averted.

Not until the next week do we get called into the principal's office. She is the flinty, affected type you would expect to be principal of an arts high school. We could be expelled for smoking pot in the lot. We deny it. We fight tooth and black-painted nail. Our mothers come in to defend us, even. The guy had said we peeled away, so Eryn's mom states the impossibility of their 20-year-old Chevy being able to peel out at all. We assert that we were smoking hand-rolled cigarettes. There is no reason to believe that, but they can't prove otherwise. This fellow we'd never seen before hadn't made any direct accusations. Who the hell is he, anyway? I cry and cry. Eryn's mom shushes me as I go overboard. I'm not being manipulative. I am sad I was caught, sad at what I am. We wind up being suspended for a week.

When I return to the school, I have to be ready to perform another song for that shitty teacher Lynn. I'd missed a week of class so should be further along with its preparation. I figure I'll be fine. She stops me after a couple of bars and tells the accompanist to play it in the key of C, and for me to make the appropriate adjustment. I ask if I could hear the new notes first. I'm not a musician, I can't read music. I can't identify notes by their corresponding letter. If she doesn't give me a chance to hear it beforehand for a bit, I will surely fail. Clearly, she *wants* me to fail. "No," she snaps, "just sing it." How the fuck am I supposed to sing it if I don't know what it sounds like. I'm not a fucking singer, I didn't come here for singing and even if I wanted to sing you are not fucking helping me. You just make it harder. None of this was in my head, you see, but all screamed at her, inches from her face. You want me to fail you fucking bitch, you stupid fucking untalented bitch.

"Get out," she says. "Gladly," I reply. I receive the call later in the day at my "regular school" that I am not to come back to BOCES the next day. I have been expelled. Other students who had said they were scared I was going to hit her, had their quotes taken out of context rendering them just "scared." This threat to student and teacher alike was enough to sign my walking papers. I am to spend the rest of the year sitting for the first part of my day at MacArthur, all alone in a cubicle for in-school suspension. At the end of the year, only a month later, I have to go back to BOCES to perform three monologues and three songs for a panel of my former teachers to determine whether or not I'll get any credit for the year I'd spent there. I haughtily return, determined to wow them with the talent they had misused. They barely acknowledge me, like I'd just shined their shoes, and that's it for me. I get credit for the year, but will not return the next. I won't graduate from acting school, I'll be thrown back in amongst everyone else for the remainder of my days. I wish it hadn't turned out this way.

Since she's a year older, I get to see Eryn graduate, though I'm not allowed on the campus. I watch her commencement from outside the fence surrounding the yard with the small amphitheater. She reads a poem that includes the line "don't drop me, like acid." That's pretty bad ass for a graduation speech. I wish I was graduating. I wish it was all over for me.

FORTY-SEVEN

I'm still communicating with my sister's roommate Brandon. We write lengthy letters of lust to one another, imagining ourselves star-crossed-cross-continental lovers. In my infinite genius – or, perhaps, desire to be discovered - I leave a half-written letter to him out on the kitchen table and go to smoke some pot in the church parking lot where I'd first tried cigarettes. Of course, mom gets home early and finds it. She is as displeased as she is disgusted. Apparently, all of his friends are giving him a hard time too. You are 23 and you hook up with your roommate's visiting 16-year-old sister? I know it's technically illegal, but it doesn't seem so bad to me. They see only the unseemly side of our union. And I don't know how my sister feels about it. If she ever says anything to him, or yells at him, we never talk about it. We don't talk about real stuff in our family.

Our forbidden love wears off soon. My mom isn't about to send me out there again and I need to focus on what is at hand. I go to the Wantagh High School junior prom with Vic D'Angelo. He is just a friend I get wasted with, but he cleaned up really nicely for the evening. With him in a tux and me in my black sequined and fringed off the shoulder dress, it is ON. I am all over him from the get go. As we all get trashed and drive around the city aimlessly in our limo, his attractiveness diminishes, replaced by goofy stoner-isms. "Smoke a bowl!" he and the other guys alternately shout and whisper, despite our having run out of pot hours before. The annoyance of this is so great that I snap at them to shut the fuck up about it. I love to smoke, but not so much to talk about it, and the fruitlessness of talking about it when it had become an impossibility is infuriating. My fury, of course, only spurs their cries. This is unwise on my date's behalf, seeing as how my sexual accessibility is contingent upon my lack of annoyance. Some laughs are the only thing he's going to get tonight.

Gina's boyfriend Scott is my age and goes to Wantagh too. He is one of Vic's friends and so it's pretty cool for us all to get to go to prom together. She is really freaking me out, though. She's been with Scott for almost a year and is still a virgin, which, as a concept, is completely alien to me. We go to a club after the gymnasium-based prom and Gina and Scott disappear. I am tripping hard. When they finally reappear, they look disheveled, and, I am convinced, deflowered. They are acting shady. I keep thinking that they had waited this long and decided to go for it in the bathroom of a club on prom night? How gross! I am really sad for her and it's giving me the creeps.

Turns out I'm wrong though. I've started thinking lots of things on acid that I am probably wrong about.

The parties that I've been going to particularly stoke my warped flights of fancy. I go with Eryn and Juliana to a big warehouse rave on the island. Juliana is a musical theater girl culled from my former place of artistic education. She is a goofy little thing, who dresses something like a hippie and is prone to eating tons of nutmeg to get high. "I'm totally 'megged!" she'll proclaim. From the time the three of us hung out and stole a bottle of Boone's farm, we were trouble. After realizing none of us had a wine opener we cracked the neck of the bottle over a rock and drank from the jagged edge. They will get along with my other friends just fine, I figure, all of us having as we do this penchant for self-abuse.

See, Rhoda and Gina are going to the warehouse party too. Gina, at my house, calls Rhoda and makes it clear she is not pleased to be going with my friends, who, as newbies, are not exactly bedecked in approved rave couture. Whatever. Gina thinks she's such hot shit lately, she goes out with Rhoda all the time. I like my new friends, and we have fun together. Yes. We are going to have fun.

I drop two tabs. $5 a pop for eight hours of fun, you can't beat the bargain, really. We dance like crazy. They are selling toys, and I buy a popgun that has a ball attached to a string, which is, in turn, attached to the gun. I could go around shooting people and then hide when the ball returns to me, so that they look around confusedly for what had struck them. Or I can shoot boys that I think are cute, and they can look at me like I am an idiot as they walk away.

I see Jason there. He gives me a smug hello and a brief, fantastical synopsis of his life as of late. I shoot him and laugh.

The night progresses. My friends and I dance gleefully. Then they fall away. Everything falls away. I am dancing with my popgun, twirling the ball on its string. I stand in the center of the arc that swirls around me, and move my hips subtly, enough to imply dancing, but not disrupt the spinning of my ball. I cannot disrupt the spinning of my ball. It seems very important. Suddenly, all the lights in the room are following my ball, and the music revolves along with it. I am at the center of a large circle. Oh my god, I realize, I am going to have to stand here and do this forever. I am stuck here spinning this ball. Maybe for eternity. No. No no no, I am not going to do that. I can stop whenever I want.

I throw the ball down before me. I hear a brief sigh of disappointment from the masses. The circle around me continues to stare briefly before moving on. A guy spins his flashlight around on the ground, on the same path my ball had taken, indicating that I should take up my charge once more. I shake my head emphatically. No. I am not going to do it anymore. I have to get out of here. We all have to get out of here. Something is going to happen. This building, this place and everything in it, all these people from my present and past, it is all going to blow. This place is going to blow the fuck up. I grab my friends hastily, pulling them through the crowd. I want to tell everyone that's in there, everyone I know, but there isn't time to find them. I get Eryn and Juliana outside and tell them why I'd extracted them. They don't argue.

"Did you see," I ask them, "Did you see what I did?" I am shaking. They hadn't. Or at least they tell me that they hadn't. They seem like they know something. I am incredulous at their denial. "All the music and the lights, for a little while," I tell them, "they were all following me. You didn't see that?"

Eryn retorts with her head down and forward, charging toward her car. "Fine, Jaime, you're special," she spits, "but I'm special too, you know, I can do cool things too. you think you're the only one with power..." she rambles on and I don't understand what she is saying. I hadn't said...I didn't mean...I get into her passenger seat. Eryn speeds away down the empty highway, lighting a bowl as we near a turn. In my mind, I see us career off the road and ask her to wait until we are stopped. She is very pissy about it. We've never been this way before. She owes me $10 for the acid. Give me $20 and I'll give you back $10 she says. Um, okay. It doesn't make sense to me, but Eryn is my friend. Yeah, sure if you say so. I had always hated math but...did my friend just rip me off? She brings me to my door.

I enter to find my mother, tense on the sofa. Where have I been? I forgot that I was supposed to have stayed over at Gina's house. Gina had said she was staying at my house. One parent had called the other, like they always seem to do. Although my eyes must be three kinds of crazy, I am not accosted for that. I'm lucky my eyes are so dark that my pupils are lost in them anyway. I apologize and shift the blame, saying Gina was drunk and I didn't want to drive with her, that I'd come home with Eryn instead. I am a fucking genius. But what was I doing until four in the morning she wants to know? Dancing. I was just dancing. It was really fun. I am sorry.

To my thinking, I am still a good kid. I do okay in school, my heart is in the right place. I am just having this tough time. Seeing the heartbreak in my mother's eyes breaks my acid-soaked heart right back. I decide that I am going to make it up to her, and that I will do so immediately. Instead of going to bed, I pull out my old box of crayons and an empty wine bottle from the trash, perhaps mom's way of dealing with my absence. I put on some music and sit for hours melting the colored wax so that it drips down the neck of the bottle. By morning, my fingers burnt and tinted, I had created a rainbow-caked monument of my intoxicated regret. In the morning, my mom accepts it thankfully, but not without concern. Then she drives me to work.

She drives me to the movie theater, one of those giant multiplexes. On the way there, I tell her of my feat the previous night with the spinning ball. I had not yet slept, and it didn't seem so crazy to me. "Oh yeah? What were you on?" she asks. She sounds like she's joking so I laugh. Nooo...I wouldn't do anything like that. I don't know why she believes me. I guess she just wants to. Just like the nights I come home high and ask her to make me two bagels with cream cheese and jelly. I'm sure she just wants to believe that I am hungry, and that she is taking care of me. I mean, in some ways, I am better. At least I'm not screaming and crying every night.

Not that I don't still have some charming episodes. I greet all the skate kids that have congregated in Gina's boyfriend's basement. He spreads his arms to give me a hug and I do the same, but then I stop, and I point at his hat. It's the Acme hat that Ron had given me. I say as much. Scott turns nasty real quick, "Fuck you, Ron said I could have it." Scott has a relationship with Ron that borders on idolatry, and he isn't going to give up that hat for anything, especially now that Ron has fled town after beating up and ripping off some big weed dealer. Tears predictably fill my eyes, as they do whenever I am not getting what I want. "He gave it to me first," I plead, "it's the only thing I have from him." "No way, fuck you," he repeats, seeming far too sensitive considering the subject matter. What can I do? I am infuriated. I lunge at his head, grabbing for my memento. He pushes me easily to the floor. "What the fuck are you doing, you crazy bitch?" he exclaims. I've just attacked the boyfriend of one of my best friends. Crazy bitch does not seem unfitting. But, then, why is it not crazy for him to hoard my hat?

And then, we go to Rhoda's one night to drink and swim in her pool, filled as we are with brilliant ideas. This one girl is saying how gross it is that she still hears her parents having sex. Everyone agrees with a groan, but I burst into sloppy, drunken tears. "At least your parents like each other," I say. I'm not trying to make her feel bad for what she said, or make people feel bad for me. It's just how I felt in that moment. I am wasted, after all. Still, the friends I'd managed to accumulate are once again growing wary of me. I am becoming a far- off island, isolated and remote.

FORTY-EIGHT

At least it seems that as lonely as I feel, I am never left alone by the fellas for too long. I start seeing Hank, another skater guy. He is cute, but his little brother is really hot. It's very distracting. I bring Hank with us to this really big rave. It's in Manhattan at a giant ballroom, the first legal venue we've attended, but with every other illicit aspect maintained. After last time's "exploding rave" incident, I think I probably shouldn't do as much acid, so I just take one. And a half.

Some pacifier-chewing stranger wearing neon and pigtails is giving out "Hello my name is _____" nametags. Hank writes "Hank's property" on mine and slaps it on my ass. I am wearing a cut off shirt with oversized jeans, and I guess look worthy of retaining. It really pisses me off, though. He proceeds to follow me around like a puppy. He never has much to say. He doesn't dance. I wish that I could shake him. I see in the corner of the room that they are projecting a Charlie Chaplin movie on a huge screen on the far wall. I'm drawn to it. The projector stands before me, its beams of light shooting forward across the room. I place my hand slowly in its stream, interjecting my hand into the story. I pat Chaplin's head, his back and his ass. I hold my thumb and forefinger together in front of the little tramp's pants, and gave him a giant, through-his-clothes hand job. Throughout the cavernous room, I hear laughter. People see what I am doing, and they like it.

The screen fades into colorful swirls, and I move the whole of my arms into the beam of light. They twist and dance upon the screen, contorting hypnotically to the music. Suddenly, the swirls are replaced by a giant record. The label in the center says "CMD welcomes new DJs." I instantly know what I am supposed to do: I put my hand on top of the record, and make like I am scratching. I get really scared that it will be linked to the music, because I have no DJ experience at all and will surely mess it up. It is a purely visual thing, though, and I faux scratch for a bit before being beset with bewilderment. "Did you see that?" I ask Hank, "when the record came on?" He had been standing right behind me. He must've seen it. "I don't know," he says, "I was really bugging out then."

Why can't – or won't - anyone confirm these feats of mine? Are they all in my head? They can't be, they are real. These things are really happening.

I am overcome with inspiration. I am great, I am special, I am somebody. As if by divine decree, someone hands me a post-it pad. I sit right down in the middle of the dance floor, writing one word on each piece, then peeling them off and throwing them aside. I am pretty sure that I'm writing something amazing, earth-shattering – unconsciously - one word at a time. I sit there for I don't know how long before my friends tell me it is time to go. They don't ask me what I am doing, surrounded as I am by the small yellow squares. I look down and realize it is a mess. Even if it is something brilliant, I'll never get it back in order. I leave the work behind to be swept up along with all the cigarette butts and little empty plastic bags. Looks like I'll be going back to the movie theater instead of onto the best-seller list.

Because my hair is black now and the shaved part is growing in, I am passable enough to work in the ticket booth. There are up to five of us at a time asking the next customer on line to please step down. My nametag says J. Andrews, and when an invariably lame old person asks if that stands for Julie Andrews, I say no, that I am going to be more famous. I'm really certain.

I like this job. Speaking through the microphone to have your voice amplified over the parking lot, smoking weed on lunch breaks, free movies and cute boys from other schools.

Hank didn't last long beyond that rave. That night was too weird and I was way too attracted to his little brother. Really, though, I should be credited for not making any moves on him. I have some standards, it seems, though the delimiters for these are uncertain, to say the least.

The movie theater is fertile ground for my amorous pursuits. The one guy who actually likes me becomes boring pretty quick, as most guys who actually like me do. I can't even kiss him. Another guy, Keith, is going out with a giant-breasted, popular girl from my high school - one of the Heathers, actually. He takes me out one night. And when I say he takes me out I mean that I fuck him in the parking lot of a mini-golf course. He says immediately afterward that he has done the other woman thing before, and it isn't for him. He made it pretty clear that this was a one-shot deal. That's fine. Whatever. I don't care.

The next week in school, I walk behind his girlfriend singing that nasty hip hop song "Boom! I fucked your boyfriend, I fucked your man..." Come on, it's a song, I am not completely responsible for the lack of class. She is no class-master herself, you know, it's rumored that she'd taken Mark Lanzer's virginity behind a bush at a keg party. My Mark Lanzer. As far as I am concerned, screwing her boyfriend is recompense for taking what I considered mine. God, who would believe that? Andrews banging the boyfriend of a Heather? What an accomplishment.

While at work, good old Al showed up at the box office with two cheesy popular girls from my school. They have bleached blond hair and are wearing combat boots as brand new as their affection for all things alternative. I haven't seen him around at all and he mumbles hello with his head down. Turns out he is dating one of them, and, I hear, living in her backyard. I don't know what that is about. I know he has friction with his parents but tent-living seems just too bizarre. However, just when I didn't think it could get any weirder, I receive a note from him via the girl he is dating.

It says only, "Et tu brute. Exit stage, right?" Now, unless he is referring to ditching him for Jason then trying to get him back - which we had resolved - I have no idea what I have done to him. I'm not going to bother to ask. I am more interested in whether or not he deliberately contorted the Shakespearean stage directions so that it became a question. If so, it was pretty clever.

But then, who needs clever? I take this big dumb jock usher behind the adjacent school after work. I get him high and suck his big dumb jock dick. Freaking idiot has to go and tell everyone, too. When we're all making fun of him in the box office one day and I take my jab, everyone gets quiet and looks at me. "He told everyone what happened," Lindsay says. Yes, the same Lindsay that beat me up and dated Mark Lanzer, briefly. I laugh it off. I don't care what they think of me. I don't care what anyone thinks. It's kind of wonderful. I approach him after work and tell him it was a shame he felt the need to share it, or maybe it could've happened again.

Fucking bitches in the box office. They deserve what I do to them. See, I have expanded my locker-shopping enterprise to my workplace. It's pretty risky and stupid of me to pilfer through their things. This isn't the wide-open expanse of a high school locker room, and it doesn't take long for management to realize that the thieving only occurs when I am working. Anyone can walk in to our walk-in closet-sized locker room at any time. But they never do. I cannot be caught. When I rip off Amanda, she has $60 in all fives. Fucking weird. *All* fives. God, maybe it's even a set up, like marking bills. When she goes on break and realizes that it's gone, she marches straight back to the box office, and walks right up to me. She wants to search my things. "Sure," I say, outwardly unfazed.

Back in the locker room, I take out my bag. "There's a bowl in the front pocket," I say casually, informing them. They don't care about that. They look in my wallet. They look in my makeup case. They look everywhere. Everywhere except the front pocket of my purse. If she had looked there, she might have found my bowl, right alongside her stack of $5 bills. She is as pissed as she is certain that I am guilty. Apparently, she really needs that money for some important life thing. Her grandmother's medication or something equally guilt-inducing, not that I allow myself to feel such things. As if it isn't bad enough for her that her name is Amanda Hunt, and that she has a brother named Michael. Apparently, he is in jail, a pretty troubled kid. Pretty much what you'd expect from Mike Hunt. Their parents must have an awesome sense of humor.

Now, one might think that I've learned a lesson now, and won't chance fate again. But naaaaah…what fun would that be? The next girl that I rip off has me take off my shoes, then my socks. Our manager stands behind her, steaming. I always act confused, helpful, innocent, all the while knowing that there is no way he is going to find me out when the cash is tucked neatly in my panties.

Oh, they must want to nail me so bad. If I am left alone in the box office, I lift a $20 from this particularly dim-witted cashier because she is always off in her till anyway. They know though, I'm sure they know.

I have to pay for my exploits somehow, and $5 an hour sure isn't going to do it. If the management knows that I do drugs, they certainly never confront me about it, even though I come to work with no sleep, or return from break wearing marijuana perfume. When a couple of guys come up to my window, a pot cloud emanating from them, I say that I'll trade some free tickets for some of what they've been smoking. It

The Brink

throws off my drawer for the night, but it's worth it.

FORTY-NINE

My bad behavior doesn't go unpunished by the universe, at least. I have awful urinary tract infections. If you've had them you know that the pain is searing, evil. You stop peeing and it feels like a mace has lodged inside of your urethra. You know you have more urine, but to release it is to revolve and expand the mace. To not release it is to have it release itself shortly afterward. I have to wear maxi-pads to catch that fluid which feels the urgent need to escape me.

Alone today in the box office with a full bladder, I know that I don't have time for anyone to rescue me. The need presents and fulfills itself almost instantaneously. I sit there and fight back the dual tears of pain and humiliation. Luckily, I'm not off for another three hours. It can dry. I just can't move from this chair. When the next shift starts coming in, I wonder if they know. If I stink. If I'll have a big darkened arc across my ass when I finally do stand. Nobody says anything, but that doesn't mean they don't know.

After a relatively long dry spell - romantically speaking - I finally meet someone at the movie theater. It isn't someone that works there this time. God knows I don't do well with men that have to deal with me on a frequent basis. I am being cross-trained and am behind the concessions stand. I don't like concessions because it is a) messier, b) sales-oriented, c) overwhelming and d) you have to STAND.

In the box office, you hit the movie they want to see, it's always basically the same price and you can't sell them anything more than the ticket. Behind the concession stand, I am too easily confused, just like tap dancing again. I can't handle the variables of candy, popcorn, and soda - to say nothing of nachos and hot dogs - plus up-selling, coupons and people pissed off that they're paying enough for a soda to pay for three bottles of the stuff. I am ineffective. Except when Darren steps up to my station. I recognize him. When I was in junior high and he was a senior at the high school next door, I'd say, "Hello, skater boy" through my bus window at him. He used to have a tuft of bleached hair in the front and skulked around in just the way I liked. He is pretty straight looking now. And hey! His friend is Andy, the guy who gave me my first hit of acid. Lookathat.

Darren eschews our obvious connection and walks off to his movie, looking back. He is seeing the late show, so I will be gone by the time he gets out. A couple of minutes later, he runs out with his phone number on a piece of paper for me. Isn't that lovely? Just like how guys are supposed to ask girls out. Of course he is going to treat me with respect, he doesn't know anything about me. I can start over fresh.

FIFTY

I am really going to get to wholly start over soon, too. The burden of bills has become too much for my underemployed father and really, he and my mother have lived in separate rooms of the same home for far, far too long to be healthy for anyone. We are selling my house, the house I've grown up in. Thank god. For years I've wanted nothing more than to get out of that school that I hate so much, that hates me so much. Before high school, we'd looked into switching school districts so that I'd be included under the - far closer - Seaford High School umbrella. My parents would have had to pay taxes for both districts, so that was nixed. I also tested and was accepted for Lutheran High, a prestigious North Shore bastion of academia, but my parents couldn't afford that either. That was such a tease. I shouldn't have even bothered testing. What would I have been somewhere else? Maybe someone entirely different. Maybe someone better. Anyway, that's a useless thought.

But now, by the new year, I will finally be in a new place, with new people. Too bad it will be halfway through my senior year. It's too late to establish myself as someone different; I already am who I am. Still, I am really looking forward to the chance.

I begin senior year at MacArthur with this renewed spirit. Both my appearance and anger have toned down considerably. All my friends have graduated, and I am now left alone in the school with all the people who've made me want to escape it. Now and then, one of them will say hi to me in the halls, un-ironically, when nobody else is around. I am shocked. It's a step. I start actually caring about what is going on in school again. I, like, *participate* and am doing really well. Don't get me wrong, I am still getting high whenever I have five minutes to spare, but it's not so distracting to me as it is edifying. I can focus, I can calm the fuck down.

I turn 17 and get my belly button pierced. You have to be 18, officially, but I go into New York and they call my mom to get permission. In theory, I could have them call anyone, but they really call my mom who really gives permission. She thinks it looks cute, and it does, if you ignore the initial purple bruise that surrounds it. The piercing makes more complete my growing penchant for wearing short shirts.

The weekends are for raves. Eryn is away at school, but then, things had gotten so weird with her anyway. Gina isn't going to school, she is just working, and I go to parties with her and Rhoda whenever I can. We flee one warehouse party in the pouring rain, tripping, laughing all the way. Then we hit an outlaw way out on the island. Outlaws are how it is supposed to be done. An abandoned warehouse that has been broken into, with the lights and speakers set up on the fly. It is dirty, it is raw - it is awesome. People are giving acid away, a party favor simply for knowing about the party. I wear a slim-fitting striped button-up shirt and carpenter pants with a wallet chain, pretty standard uniform. My top and bottom buttons are undone symmetrically, to reveal my new piercing.

The music is dark and the vibe is intense. As I dance, a stranger walks by with a glow-stick on a chain. He hands it to me. I know what I am supposed to do. I wonder if he does, too. I start to swing the stick from the end of the chain. This is far superior to the ball on a string that I'd used before. As I revolve my hand gently, the path of the glow stick causes a phosphorescent green orb to be etched in the air at the end of the chain. The people gather, entranced. This time I can handle it. This time I relish it. I move my hips in concert with the light lasso that I twirl around me.

The chain gets caught on my thumb and the light falls to

the ground, inert, just as the music in the venue screeches to a halt. What - how? I can't help but feel responsible. I pick up the slack and start swinging again. The beats do as well, but I trip up quick and the music, once again, stops. The whole room groans. I begin again, determined not to let everyone down, not to let the music stop. It's at least ten minutes, twirling, twirling. Someone intercepts the light's path. It stops and again, the music does too. This time I hear a shout from the front of the room, where the turntables are. "If you mother fuckers don't chill the fuck out, I'm going to shoot all of y'all."

Okay. I'm not going to start up again. I'm too scared of what could happen the next time I stop. I step outside where more revelers litter the overgrown field. I feel a sting and look down. On the outside of my right hand's index finger, several layers of flesh have been worn away by the friction of the revolving chain. It oozes, shiny and pink. It burns. I light a cigarette and walk to my friends. I ask if they know what the hell had gone on in there. "Yeah," they say, "two guys were fighting up by the DJ." Apparently, they kept hitting the tables and finally Frankie Bones, who was spinning, threatened to kill them if they did it again. "Wow," I say. I don't tell them how I might have controlled what occurred, I know better than to bring that stuff up anymore. Still, raves are supposed to be about peace and love and all that shit. "It's over," I inhale on my cigarette, referring to the scene. "It's over."

FIFTY-ONE

Now, yes, I am dating Darren, but my teenage libido is never hampered by such restrictions. As I leave the party, my eyes meet their match. He is a rave Malcolm McDowell, with the requisite blonde Caesar haircut. His heavy jaw juts forward with the weight of ecstasy, and his ice blue eyes melt me. "Hello," he says with a swagger, his lips parted. "Hi," I reply, holding his gaze. "Where are you off to?" the swagger holds through to his voice, thick with a British accent. Mmmph, perfect. "I gotta go, but I'm going to be at Motion next week," I offer hurriedly, my friends already in Gina's car. "I'll be there," says English man with a wink as he walks away. Whoo! WHOO-HOO! I am in love. Maybe the scene isn't dead just yet. Heck, I am just getting started. I was supposed to have been home by two and it's five. Nobody is awake, but when I get into my room, I see mom has ripped all my posters off the walls. That's fine. I start putting up rave flyers in their stead.

I doodle the names of DJs and raves on my notebooks, each word surrounded by percussive waves. My social studies buddy Louis, one of maybe three black guys in the whole school, writes mocking retaliatory names under each of the DJ's I herald. Frankie Bones meets Sammy Skeleton. On-E is flanked by Under-D, etc. I am having a pretty good time.

I even still have Darren, who assures that on nights that I am not out getting wasted, I am at least getting laid. He is pretty straight, really. He drinks, but isn't into weed or anything. It's a nice balance. I have my movie theater job, amazingly enough, and now I have my license. Mom works pretty much around the block, so I can take her to the bank in the morning and bring her car to school and work. Permission, however, isn't a necessity for taking out the Camry. "Cammy's Camry."

I find myself strangely without pot and desperate, so, after mom goes to bed, I drive up a half hour to Juliana's to get my fix. Juliana's parents are Russian immigrants. They'd bought a big home in one of Long Island's most prestigious neighborhoods, but it stands like an empty shell. It doesn't have the opulent furnishings, impeccable landscaping and two luxury vehicles of the surrounding homes. I'm not even sure how they afford the home in the first place, as it seems to me that all her parents ever do is sit at home and drink from a large jug of cheap wine. They have their vices, and so scolding Juliana for hers is wholly ineffectual.

It's half past midnight when I leave. The Seaford-Oyster Bay Expressway is spread out lonely and vacant before me. I like to drive fast, and I wonder just how fast this baby can go. How fast I can go. The road's subtle turns challenge me as my speedometer rises. "I bet…" I think, "…I bet I could go 100 miles an hour!" I press down still harder on the gas, and the trees beside me became a green blur as I traverse suburbia. Deep dark trance music blares from the stock stereo system. It's like I could take flight, right there.

Then they appear, the flashing lights behind me. My eyes widen and my mouth dries as I look into my rearview in horror. I am in pretty deep shit. Not just high now, but the music and the lights and the stress push me into a flashback, or reignite the previous weekend's acid. I feel my eyes become giant revolving discs. As the officer approaches my window, I rub at my mouth, which crumbles away.

"I am supposed to be home at midnight," I stammer. "I fell asleep studying," I lie. "I'm so sorry." I mean that. I am always sorry to be caught. I've had my license for less than a month. The first six months of your license are probationary. If that cop decides to bust me, I'll be without a license until I am 21. He doesn't. I am lucky. So, so lucky.

The Brink

I am squandering the normal human allotment of luck on such situations. My good fortune seems to be solely based on the capacity to get out of the messes I get myself into. It doesn't help with my feelings of superiority. No sir, I am untouchable. The key is to never take it for granted that all will turn out well. If you really believe each time is the one you are going down, providence will step in.

FIFTY-TWO

Baker from the movie theater is having a party. His name being an apt descriptive, I go because I am sure I'll be able to get high there. I walk in and the guys flock to me. Whether my reputation preceded me, I do not know, maybe they think I'll be doling out some blow jobs. Either that or it just seems as though dudes surrounded me because no female coworkers will speak to me, seeing as how I've robbed them all at some point. Perhaps it's just one of those nights where my vibe is high. Such evenings are always matched by evenings when no guy will so much as look at me, so that keeps me at least somewhat humble. Nobody is getting high, though. I am itching for it, and start asking around. To my rescue steps a longhaired loser who looks like a reject from a hair-metal band of the previous decade. He lives right around the corner, and has some pot there. Awesome.

I ascend the stairs to his single room with sloping ceiling and rock poster wallpaper. He has just one chair, and I sit in it. He rolls a joint and we smoke it. "Thanks," I say, "let's go back." He wants me to hold on a second, though. I am so hot, he says, as he sits on the arm of the chair that I am in and caresses my head. He leans in to kiss my cheek.

My body feels alert yet paralyzed. "Sorry," I say, "I have a boyfriend." Darren is, on occasion, convenient to recall. He asks why I came to his house, then. I think I'd made my reason for doing so abundantly clear. That aim had been achieved. He rolls off the arm of the chair and on to me. His whole body presses down on me like a dentist's lead x-ray smock. I sit frozen. I don't push him away as he kisses my neck and face, though my chin is averted. "Will you please stop?" I say firmly, "please, can we go back to the party?" He keeps kissing me and I think, "Jesus, this is it. I have done this, this is my fault, I'm so stupid." He is going to rape me, maybe he will kill me. Tears stream out of my eyes. I become more insistent. "For real, fucking stop!" I cry. I guess it hits him what is going on, I am not just playing hard to get. He eases his weight off of me and I spring up and dart down the stairs to the door. It is locked from the inside and I press against it until he meets me at the bottom of the stairs with the key. So lucky, I am so lucky.

He releases me into the night and I run back to the party. I clean off my tears and find Baker. "Who's your long-haired friend," I ask him. "Just a neighbor," he replies. "He's a fucking asshole," I say, ignoring the fact that he could've been a far greater asshole than he was. Then I leave, so thankful that providence has stepped in once more. I don't tell anyone about it, because if I did so, I would have to include the fact that I went to a strange dirt-bag's house to get high. The whole experience killed my buzz, too. It would've served me right if the worst had happened.

FIFTY-THREE

We are close to selling the house. Someone is interested, a young couple. I wonder if they know how totally shitty, and capable of destroying the will of children, our local school district is. I come into the house after my matinee shift to find my mom and dad at the underused dining table with a stranger. He is the realtor and has a stack of papers. They tell me to sit down. It is final. We'll be out of here by December first. The anniversary of losing my virginity. I don't know why the fuck they are telling me. Why are they including me? It isn't my fucking house, I hate this place, do whatever the fuck you want. In a show of restrained rebellion, I go to the front door, open it and throw my drinking glass out on the steps, smashing it. I'd needed to smash something, and really should have been commended for having the presence of mind to smash it in an easily remedied location. Though I must admit, not simply dashing it against the fireplace certainly lessened the dramatic thrust of the gesture. I don't know why I got so mad. I thought I couldn't wait to get out of this place. Huh.

It isn't much longer now and I'll get what I've always wanted: away. Before I leave, I decide to ask this girl, Jessie, to come to a party with me. Jessie Asbury. I don't really go out with Gina and Rhoda anymore. The last time I had, they shoved me in the backseat of the Stealth and disparaged me. "Ravers are so snotty,' Rhoda said. "It's true, ravers are such assholes!" agreed Gina. "I don't think I'm an asshole," I chirped. Rhoda and Gina traded glances "That's because you're not one," Gina said frostily. She didn't mean that I wasn't an asshole, she meant that I wasn't a raver. She'd been to maybe five more parties than me. If that made her a raver, then yeah, she was an asshole.

I love how the people who eschewed the popular crowd

in high school are establishing the same hierarchy in this rave-world microcosm, and with even more strict standards. Forget that, man, I've had enough. I also love how, despite my rampant lies, thievery, drug use and philandering, I still don't consider myself an asshole. Nonetheless, I enjoy parties, and I'll go and have fun regardless of whom I am with. So, I ask Jessie.

She isn't anybody. I mean, she is a nice girl, but really under the radar. Our lockers have been placed next to each other for four years due to the marvels of alphabetical order, but I've somehow managed never to speak with her before. She said she would come to a NASA party with me and Juliana.

I am wearing these black and white striped overalls I just got that I'd been looking for everywhere. With a black baby tee underneath, I look like some kind of slutty, test-pattern train conductor. Juliana has just given herself a big rave-makeover. She's gotten her eyebrow pierced and wears matching oversized shirt and jeans with the amusingly named Fuct label. It's a skate company, but I wouldn't be surprised to hear it was a demarcation for all of our kind. Truly, we were all pretty Fuct.

I buy two hits of acid from Mark, this creepy guy that Gina has a big crush on. She and Rhoda are there, but we speak only cursorily. I'm sure they are making fun of me and my green-to-the-scene friends. I don't care. I hear that Rhoda's hot boyfriend Tom Sparks just robbed her. She had him arrested and he got sent to rehab. I guess she's right about ravers being assholes, huh?

On the bright side, the acid is yellow sunshine, really strong hits that have been going around. Excellent. On-E is spinning tonight too, he is my favorite. He's just been picked up by the band Deee-lite and is being forced to change his name to Ani under pressure from the record label to disperse the drug allusions that so entices the community they are courting. On-E plays the heaviest stuff, which I really like, even though it freaks me out. The beat is sharp and high-pitched…were it Morse code it would look like _ _ .. _ _ _/_ _ .._ . _ _ over and over and over again. It makes my eyes widen and jaw clench, or maybe that's the drugs. It makes me feel like something is going to happen, a dark but thrilling anticipation. I look everywhere for English man, who'd stirred my fancy some weeks earlier, but I haven't seen him since.

However, as I dance, "Super Dave" sidles up to me, dancing and looking at me out of the corner of his eye. He is like a rave celebrity, for crying out loud. I really feel like a part of something. Something big, really big. He asks if Jessie, Juliana and I want to retreat into the back room to smoke a bowl. Jessie doesn't want any weed. She hadn't done any acid either, but she was still managing to act really fucked up. She looks like she is going to die. "Are you alright?" I ask her quietly. She looks at me, piqued and sheepish. "Gas," she says quietly and waves her hand around. This fills me with horror. What the fuck is she thinking just sitting there and farting away? Juliana keeps asking, in reference to her new rave-alicious outfit, "Is this me? But do you think it's me?" "How can I answer that?!" I shout. We have to get out of there, out, out, out again. Immediately.

With some forethought or guidance, I may have deemed this an unwise decision. It is 3am, which means we've just missed the last trains out to Long Island. We would have to wait there, in the Long Island Rail Road station waiting room, until 5:30am. As we enter the station, an old homeless man with the tiniest of kittens sits at the foot of the elevator. He has three of them. I gasp loudly and plunge my hand into my backpack. I withdraw a $5 bill and give it to the man. "You take care of them," I plead with him, ignoring the fact that he is likely as hungry as they are. We continue our descent to the holding pen.

It is an assortment of drunks and disorderlies. For the

most part, the room is populated by men that look like they've remained in the outfits they socially peaked in ten to thirty years before. There are 80s guys and disco kings, still holding on to their former glory. One of them wears an Adidas tracksuit. I want one of those so bad. I tell him how cool it is and he looks at me angrily. I guess he thinks I am making fun of him but I really meant it, Adidas tracksuits are totally cool.

Something important is going on. I can feel it. I am gonna get the current issue of "Backstage." Either there is an undercover director in this grim holding cell, just waiting to discover me, or this issue of "Backstage" will contain a casting call for the role that will finally make me a star. Finally. Clearly that's what has to happen. Everything is just too intense for it not to happen. He who hath in himself no chaos, hath no power to create a star! I search through the paper, desperately reading, looking for the ad that describes me. The Adidas man and his friend are making fun of me, I know it. An adorable rave kid enters the room. He's forgotten about the last train too. He will be our friend. We move into a corner in a huddle on the floor.

I feel great, but every time I look at Jessie, she looks like she is about to die. Of course, I feel responsible. She has to use the bathroom, but the waiting room bathrooms are closed for repairs. All the restaurants in the station are closed. Everything is closed, it's the middle of the night. Then I look at Jessie and she looks great, but *I* feel like I am going to die. It keeps shifting. She really has to go. She is going to have to leave the station. One of us is going to have to go with her. I don't want to be left alone. I don't know this cute boy. I don't know that I can trust him. I will go outside with Jessie.

We ascend the escalators back into the relatively still city night and look around for a point of relief. The lights of a hotel and chain restaurant gleam across the street. To me, the street may as well be an ocean teeming with sharks. There is no way to cross it safely - the traffic light is somehow not a consideration as the cars seem to ceaselessly flow. Jessie has to go, she is going to cross. I beg her not to risk it. She tells me that she has no choice. I will not join her. No way. She turns to the homeless man with the kittens and asks him to watch me. "Well, alright!" he exclaims, glad to be of service. And she hadn't done drugs? She is about to leave me in the care of a homeless man while she attempts to cross the street, an act that, from my perspective, can only end in her demise. She starts to run across as the cars rush onward, honking. I can't look. I go back downstairs to Juliana.

"Where's Jessie?" she asks me. "She's gone," I respond, ominously. I mean it in the most final of ways. When she returns a couple of minutes later, I am astounded.

Our train will finally be coming in 15 minutes. We amble toward the big screen where our track number will be revealed. I then realize that I'd forgotten my copy of "Backstage" in the waiting room. I have to go back to get it. Leaving it in there would be tantamount to dismissing any possibility of a career. A symbol, you see. Everything is symbols. But I have to get on the train. The train I've been waiting for all this time. The train that will take me away. I walk toward the waiting room, then turn around to walk back to the board. I do it again. And again. I repeat my tight concentric circles, wild-eyed, and fully driven on my divergent purposes. Everything else has fallen away. I don't know where my friends are

A police officer with outdated hair approaches me. "Are you alright?" he asks. Here he is! The undercover director, he's found me! This is it. "You're looking for an actress," I assert, my finger toward his face. "No," he replies, repeating, "are you alright?"

No. I've been all wrong. Clearly, I am all wrong. My location and circumstances flood over me, my friends are around me again. He repeats his question once more. "Are you alright?"

"No," I say. "I'm not alright. Something's wrong, something's very wrong." "Okay," he says, "what do you want?" An invisible audience holds its breath in anticipation of my response. I don't know, it must be a code. What equals safety, comfort? Mother, I want my mother. "You want us to call your mom?" he asks. Yes. "Yes," I say.

Juliana holds her head down and shakes it emphatically. "She's fine. She's FINE," her shrill nasal voice barks. It cuts right through me. "No," I argue, "I'm not fine at all." I'm not. I don't know what is wrong but something definitely is. I want it to stop. "Jaime come on, the train is here,' Juliana pleads.

"Do you want to go on the train?' asks Officer Hill Street Bluesman, "does that sound like a good idea?"

I guess it does. Yeah. The train, we've been waiting for the train. But, why did the cop ask me that? Is it not a good idea? Does he know something? He should know, he's a cop. He represents the order I so desperately want in my mind.

"Come on, Jaime, c'mon." The way Juliana says it sounds evil. How am I supposed to trust that? She must be trying to destroy me. If I get on this train, I am going to die. "Can I go on the train?" I ask the cop. "Yeah," he replies, "yeah, why don't you go on the train." I'm not sure how to feel about that. His voice drips with the unstated. It is almost like a dare. I'll try it, sure...sure...the train isn't going to kill me, that's ridiculous.

I go down the stairs to the platform. Descending them mirrors the descent into hell, and the temperature even rises to confirm that feeling. It's a difficult situation to trust. I enter the train and sit down with my friends around me. "See? This is good, see? You're on the train! Good girl," Juliana purrs. The officer sticks his head through the doorway. "Are you sure you're alright? You're alright on the train?"

No, no, no, no, I'm not. He is right, something is very wrong. This train leaving represents my death. I am not going to fall for that, no. I don't want to die. I jump over the back of the seats in front of me and scramble out the door and up the stairs. My friends are close behind me.

"Can I go?" Jessie asks the officer. She wants to go home on the train by herself and he lets her. Whatever, let her go, clearly she isn't making the best decisions this evening. She runs off down the stairs. "You sure you don't want to go too?' he asks. Everyone looks at me expectantly. "C'mon," the adorable raver boy says to me, flirtingly, "let's get on the train." "Oh yeah?" I reply suggestively, following him as he backs toward the stairs, "Yeah, he says, "c'mon, it'll be cool." I stop dead in my tracks. I see what they are doing, attempting to use sex to lure me. Nice try, but I am too smart for that.

"No. NO." I shout. He scurries off on his own. I look back at the cop and Juliana standing there. "Last chance," they tell me. "Last call for the Babylon branch," blares throughout the station. It doesn't help that the name of my train line is biblical in origin. A bell sounds as the train kicks into gear, chugging its way out of the station. The sound is that of a soul departing.

"Up, there it goes," the officer says. "We missed it," fumes Juliana. "You missed your train," says the officer portentously. Oh. Oh, I blew it. The dread washes over me. I was wrong. I was supposed to get on the train! Now I missed it. I missed it and it is over. I am – am I dead? I don't know. I have to find my way back.

"C'mon," the officer says. He leads me and Juliana to the police office within the station and hands me off to the man in charge there. The officer behind the counter is giant, likely elevated by some sort of platform to make perps feel small.

Name? He asks me. Jaime Andrews, I am Jaime Andrews. Address? Phone number? I feverishly rattle off my information, the code he needs to unlock the secret of me. I give the names of my friends. Juliana Abramoff, Jessie Asbury. I have it figured out. Both of their names are steps to get to mine. Juliana Abramoff, Jessie Asbury, Jaime Andrews.

I repeat my address, I repeat my phone number. I need to get the code right so I can get back. Back to reality from this other universe that I have clearly passed into at some point during this crazy, crazy night. The officer steps into another room. I shout my code at him, trying to secure my way back to normalcy. He returns with another giant officer and a wheelchair. "We're going for a little ride and your mom will meet you there."

Yeah?!? Really?!? Great! Great, great, great! I win! I am going to be okay! It's really amazing. I look at the officer's nametag. It is comprised of all consonants. Clearly he is an usher in this monstrous purgatory, and he is going to lead me out. "Hop on," he says. "You're going to wheel me there?" I am incredulous. "Yeah, top treatment," he scoffs. Unbelievable! I have not only saved myself, but I don't even have to walk to get wherever we are going. I am a princess, relieved, on top of the world.

"In that case," I say, reaching into my bag. I finish my sentence by taking out a cigarette and lighting it as he wheels me through the cavernous station. Being wheeled back to sanity, I can finally relax. "No, you can't do that," he says. "I can though," I retort, "I'm doing it right now, look!" I inhale deeply as he wheels me along. Officer No-vowels plucks my fag from my fingers and tosses it aside. "No, you can't," he replies playfully. I moan in comedic disappointment. Okay. Fine. This is still pretty great.

He wheels me out the door with Juliana trotting beside

me. There is an ambulance waiting. I'm going in the ambulance? I really can't believe it. All this special attention! "Are you putting the siren on?" I ask. "No, no," he says, greeting another officer waiting inside. "Can you get up," he asks me. "Sure, yeah!" I chirp. I rise from the chair to step up into the back of the ambulance.

"Sure, she can get up,' oozes the officer inside. "I'll bet she can," says officer no-vowel. Huh? They spend the ride barraging us with innuendos that confuse and disturb us.

"Look at you sitting there all cute," they say, "you think you're cute sitting there with your hands in your lap?" "You always keep your hands in your lap."

"In a lap, right?"

Uh, right. They are the officers, they are in charge, they are the ones on the right side of the law. Whatever they say, yeah. I'm not in a position to argue. They bring me to St. Vincent's hospital downtown. I'm taken to some ward and put in a bed. I keep moving the curtain that separates me from my neighbor. I'm sure he wants to talk to me though, apparently, he is unconscious. The doctor asks me questions, gives me pills and juice and a cookie. I sit there as they serve me. It's fantastic! Suddenly, my mother appears in the doorway. There she is! I start laughing hysterically. She looks scared though, I guess she doesn't get it.

I am wheeled into a small room by a man wearing street clothes. I'm not sure what is going on, or who he is. He starts to close the door. What are they doing? Why are they letting this man be alone with me in here? I am so scared that I scream and scream. I scream bloody murder. I scream at the top of my lungs. It is a blood-curdling scream. All of those. No, No! Get away from me, get away from me. This is the last thing that I remember before I fall asleep.

When I wake up later, Juliana and mom are still there.

"How are you feeling?" they ask. Fine, I am fine. "Oh shit, I guess I fucked up, huh?" I laugh. They don't. "Yeah, Jaime, that was really bad," Juliana says, bitchily. Mom can't really talk. She looks like she's been lobotomized. The doctor comes in to check up and check out. "Someone came by to see how you were feeling," the doctor says, ushering in officer no-vowel. He has vowels now. Not many, it is one of those giant Polish names, Wcyswienski or something. I swear those vowels weren't there before. I point at him and wag my finger, saying something to the effect of, "Aheeeeeh...," which is a direct translation of, "I see what you did there." He asks if I am going to be a good girl from now on. I promise, as coquettishly as the request requires. I don't say anything like, "Hey, you totally fucked with my head!" Who would believe me? I'd fucked with my own head, and whatever happened while I was in that state was as unverifiable as it was unlikely. That's a shame too, because I am starting to have all these questions that nobody seems to be able to answer. I ask Juliana if the cops had been messing with us and she does verify that much. Sure, she'd dropped a hit too, but at least it wasn't all just in my head.

Mom, Juliana and I walk the almost-20 blocks back to Penn station from St. Vincent's. Juliana boards the train back to Syosset, and mom and I take the one back to Seaford. She is close-lipped while I apologize. Finally, she breaks. Why would I do these things when I had so many problems already? This sort of thing wouldn't help me emotionally...and what if I'd stayed that way? Never came back from the trip I was on? I've heard of people like that. Guys that took too much acid and now think that they are oranges, sitting around hospital wards trying to peel themselves. She is right. I don't know why I did it. I am sorry. I won't do it again. I've learned my lesson. That's what I tell her.

I am really embarrassed to see Jessie at school after that.

I apologize and she tells me it was fine. But when she looks at me, it's with fear in her eyes. Luckily there is only one more week left in that place. Just one more week.

FIFTY-FOUR

I go to work at Loews for the last time. It is someone else's last day too, and they get a cake and a card that everyone has signed. I've been working there just as long, but I don't get anything. I feel hurt for a bit, but don't kid myself. I know I don't deserve anything.

Nonetheless, I have the temerity to approach my manager and ask for a transfer to the theater close to where I'll be living. "We think you should move on," he says, in the firmest voice a 25-year-old with excessive management training courses can muster. I acquiesce, and in doing so, admit to my every transgression that they hadn't been able to prosecute. Theoretically, if they hadn't been able to fire me for something, they should be able to refer me. What am I going to do, argue? I don't have it in me anymore. We all know the truth. I'd gotten away, and now I should just go away. Fine.

FIFTY-FIVE

Mom and I find an apartment in Hauppauge. Folks call it Happy Hauppauge, with varying degrees of sarcasm, depending on the source. For example: the realtor = wholly sincere, the local teens = not so much. The first time we drive around the area, I see a 10-year-old skate boarder and get excited because I know that where there are little ones, there are bound to be bigger ones.

There is one thing I am sure that I have to do before I leave Levittown, however, and that is Mark Lanzer. Last year he'd told Gina, since they were neighbors and their sisters best friends, that he would sleep with me but he "doesn't want to do that to me." I appreciate his respectfulness and all, but really, I want him to do that to me. It's not that he is a pillar of virtue. There was that bush-with-Heather thing, and everyone knew he'd nailed Vera Langdon on an air conditioner behind 7-11. Why they were worthy of his loveless thrusting, and not me, I don't know. I guess it's because he knows I am crazy, knows I'll make it into something more than it is. There is no reason for him to think that, considering I've never given problems to any of my other temporary paramours. However, though I claim to know it wouldn't mean anything, I feel such a connection with Mark that I'm sure - were he to finally give in to me - the experience would be so magical that he'd never let me go. I let him know my time in that school is almost up and he says we should hang out. It is going to happen this time. Finally.

Yeah, I am still with Darren, but I have that figured out. We aren't married…I just have to be honest with him. Because honesty, apparently, is so important to me. So, I go to my boyfriend and I tell him that, if given the opportunity, I want to be with someone else. He has to understand, it's just built up for so long. He does not bear the news with the equanimity I had hoped for. Conversely, he becomes quite angered. Go figure. He doesn't end it with me though, he curtly tells me that I am free to do what I please.

I am ready. Mark never calls though, and I don't call him. I'm not going to beg. Darren had made me feel so filthy about my intended betrayal, but not half as filthy as did Mark's denial of my virtual proposition. I save face by telling Darren that I'd not been able to go through with it because I cared about him too much. So much for all that honesty.

FIFTY-SIX

I have only two days of classes left at Mac Arthur. Crazy. My whole life with these people, and soon it will be over. I bring my camera to school and I take pictures of all the people who have been even slightly pleasant to me. Two younger skater kids I get high with sometimes, Louis who always made fun of my rave DJ's, the kids who sit next to me in math class --

"Who took that picture?" Mrs. Prince wheels around in a fury, her over-retirement age voice roaring with a quality previously unheard. I've taken math class with her for three years of high school. She is a fine old broad, never bothered me none.

Well, she'd been pretty pissed two years before when I opted for reading instead of paying attention in her Sequential 3 class. I hate math, always have, and when I couldn't grasp the concepts of a squared minus 2x and blah blah blah, and realized I didn't have to pass in order to graduate, well, I figured I might as well spend the time wrestling with concepts that better agreed with me. She made me bring back to her a letter signed by my mother stating that she was aware that I was reading "The Tao of Pooh" rather than performing those useless equations. Still, in my senior year, with a full day of classes to configure, I thought I'd take another whack at the math thing. Now I am the slower senior in the class with accelerated juniors, two of whom I was photographing when Mrs. Prince's bellow rang out across the room.

Everyone looks at me and I admit with confusion that I had been the origin of the flash that went off. "Give me that camera!" she screeches. Mrs. Prince darts toward me in a manner far spryer than one would expect from a woman pushing 75. I don't understand as she approaches me, arms outstretched. "Give it to me, give it to me!" she demands. I refuse. As she nears, I thrust the camera inside my shirt. Why the fuck does she want my camera? Why the fuck is she attacking me? Her arms encircle me and she fixes me with a possessed glare. "I'll go get it," she hisses through clenched teeth. "Go ahead," I dare her. The class stares in shock at the two of us grappling. I turn my head from within its lock. "Will someone please do something?" I implore of the gaping onlookers. Mrs. Prince just keeps grabbing at me, her arm by my face. "I'll bite you, I'll bite you," I threaten. I am just trying to get her off of me, I'm not really going to bite her. The vice principal walks in; I guess someone had retrieved her. "What's going on here?" she asks, predictably. Mrs. Prince drops her hold on me and walks to the front of the room and I dissolve into just-as-predictable tears. "Jaime, come outside please?" the veep says sternly. "I didn't do anything...I didn't do anything," I mutter as I walk out with my head down. I really hadn't this time.

We walk to the vice-principal's office, me crying all the way. I tell her the story and she informs me that Mrs. Prince has a skin condition that makes her look spotty when photographed. How could I have possibly known that? "I didn't even take a picture of her," I exclaim. No matter, they are going to have to take my camera. I complain that I've only taken five pictures so far, and I am taking pictures of the friends that I am leaving behind in only two days. I don't want a picture of Mrs. Prince and I hadn't tried to take one. They are going to develop the pictures and see for themselves. They will get me new film, per my demand. I am to go home. I am suspended. Yet again.

But, why am I suspended? She should be suspended, she attacked me. "She asked for your camera, and you didn't give it to her," they counter. That is insubordination. I'd learned enough by now to know that arguing with the powers that be is a useless pursuit. I leave. So, it turns out THIS is my last day at Mac Arthur.

They mail us the pictures and, just as I'd said, there isn't one of Mrs. Prince. There is also no new roll of film, and, of course, no apology. It is a fitting end, really.

FIFTY-SEVEN

First day at a new school, first time as a new kid. I am an "apartment kid" now, like my ex-boyfriends had been, and which had seemed so alien to me at the time.

The school newspaper is distributed on the day I get there. I leaf through it and spot a record review section. In it is a review of Smashing Pumpkins' "first album" "Siamese Dream." I scoff and turn to the girl next to me. "This chick's an idiot," I say, "their first album was 'Gish.'"

"That's my best friend," the girl replies haughtily. Of course she is. A thousand people in this school and I aim my mockery at the best friend of the girl I'm mocking. "Well...she should do a little research before she writes something." I say undaunted, though I am. These two girls will clearly not be amongst my new friends.

So how do you meet people? Common ground. And what's a common ground amongst teenagers? Drugs. I start asking where the pot is so fast that I am sure people will think I am a Narc. But no, I guess I look too much like an actual pothead to seem like a Narc. I make friends right away. Weed, the great unifier! There is no smoking it on campus though, hell no. Actual security guards crawl all over the place. If you so much as move suspiciously in the courtyard, you will see one of them ease over toward you to get a better view, let you know you are being watched. You can't even have cigarettes on campus. This is going to be tough.

But it's like I am an exotic bird here, and I am flocked to by those in the school who are perhaps seeking their own new starts. It's just like when Vera Langdon got to our school in 8th grade. Friendless as I was, and charming as she seemed, I befriended her right away. She was quickly led to an illustrious life of keggers and air-conditioner sex by those more popular than I, but it certainly helped me understand who it was that was drawn to me now: the misfits, hoping to find the understanding in me that they hadn't found in four years at Hauppauge High School.

The first girl to talk to me is Cheyenne. She is a pretty blonde with a trashy mouth. She introduces me to her rag tag crew of bland Long Island girls, but she clearly has a wilder streak that belies her association with them. Ryan starts talking to me right away too. He wears old vintage clothes and has puffy pinkish hair that makes him look like a gay-pride Q-tip. He is in my film class.

Yeah, what the hell, they have a film class complete with an editing and recording studio! I am taking a creative writing class too, and, though it is too late to become involved now, there is a fully operational radio station and everything. It is pretty amazing. I can't help but wonder what my life would be like if I'd gone to a school like this a long time ago. Not just because of the interesting classes, but because it is physically impossible to engage in my myriad vices while on campus. This is not to say that I don't try. What are limitations there for, if not to challenge them?

I learn that one can occasionally get away with a cigarette in the girls' room, but it is not something you want to chance frequently. All enjoyment is sapped when one is sucking away furtively, in fear of being discovered. I prefer to relax, like I can in my own living room.

So, I sit in the stall alone after lunch and am met there by a teacher on patrol for my kind. It's to the office with me, and I get my first detention in my new school. I am so pissed off that I go back down to the bathroom to finish my smoke, only to be met by the same broad. I laugh and sigh. I suggest that it shouldn't even count because it is the same cigarette, but she doesn't care. I wonder if she gets some kind of bonus for meeting a quota. I return to the office for my second detention. I'd never had detention in Mac Arthur, only suspension. How is that possible? I guess they didn't want to keep me around there any longer than was necessary.

I am not making the best of impressions upon the administration. I am lost in the classes. Either we are being taught what I'd already learned or the curriculum is entirely different. Damn. And I'd been doing so well for a minute there. I discover that I'm not even going to have a yearbook. They already completed the Hauppauge one, and the Mac Arthur is just getting started. That's a shame too, because if I'd stayed at the latter, I would've surely been voted "Most Interesting." That's the class euphemism for "biggest freak." I wouldn't mind that. It's nice to excel at something, and it would also be nice to be branded as interesting, even if that wasn't the intended implication. Kelly Kahn won the title - the girl I'd stolen the weed from - and let me tell you, she isn't very interesting.

What would I do with a yearbook from Hauppauge anyway? It would be filled with people I don't know and signed emptily by the few I'd had time to meet. I might as well not exist.

So, who better to validate my presence than the local men-folk? Within the first week my target is spotted. Chris goes to Central Islip, or "CI," the nearby school on the wrong side of the tracks, literally, south of them. Chris is a huge pothead, so the two of us are a natural match. I only meet him because he already has a girlfriend at Hauppauge. She is nice too, so I almost feel bad that I am going to have to put an end to their union. See, Chris looks a lot like Jason, just with some more meat on him. He even wears the same Notre Dame hat.

Oh, yeah...Darren is still around, but the drive to me now takes twice as long, so I see him half as much. Plus, I have other priorities. I am still going out to parties all the time.

After the Penn Station incident, mom didn't want me going out anymore, but there isn't any stopping me at this point. I have a key to her car, after all. When she says I can't go out, I hold up her key and assure her that I most certainly can. And I do. I drive out of the apartment complex shaking with adrenaline.

When I get to Juliana's house, her mother opens the door and, seeing me, starts to close it again, emitting a nasal whine. Juliana's mom acts not unlike some sort of savant. I knock again. "No, no...," I hear her say through the door. She opens it again, her head down, "No. No...Juliana can't go out." Her father shouts bearishly from inside, "Is it the druggist? Go away druggist!" I laugh. The druggist? I am the druggist. Awesome.

Juliana's mom continues. "She can't go out until she gives me back my wine. She took my wine."

"I'll give you your wine when you give me back my bowl, ma!" Juliana shrieks from upstairs. They yell at each other as Juliana trots down the stairs and toward the door, thrusting the half empty jug into her mother's arms. "Here, here, freak, now give me my bowl." The exchange is made, and Juliana pushes her way out the door, slamming it in her mother's face.

"Man!" she says, shaking her head. I look at her incredulously, "Jesus Christ!" We crack up. That was fucking amazing. We get into mom's car, light a pre-rolled joint to relax, and into Manhattan we go. It's winter, and the ground is covered with snow and ice. The city of the early 90s is a dingy, sketchy place, but we are unphased by its dangers. We park on the industrial west side, passing hookers on the way. They are wearing thongs! Thongs on the street in the middle of winter! Fantastic. We leave mom's car and walk around the corner, headed to Motion. It has been going on every Friday for months. It was where English man had said he was going to be that one time. If he was there, I hadn't seen him, but I'm not done looking. We pass the entrance to another club and I slip on a patch of ice right onto my ass. The bouncer at the door throws his head back as he points and laughs.

We prove ourselves worthy of further mockery when we arrive at Motion only to discover that it's been shut down. I don't know why we hadn't heard about the closure. I suspect they are all inside, laughing at the little girls that stand freezing and confused in the doorway.

We aren't about to give up that easily, not after the fight we'd both had to get out of our houses. We return back to the island, but brought the party to Caffeine, the Long Island rave club. I'd never taken it as seriously as a city club - partially because two guys from my old high school had started it - but it turns out that Caffeine is really a great place. Two huge dance spaces, lots of areas to chill and a big backyard with a shelled-out VW bus in which various illicit substances are smoked as if to commemorate the vehicle's hippie roots.

Juliana starts talking to this bleachy-haired rave kid, a Caffeine promoter named Ted. He sells drugs and she tells me he's really dumb. What the fuck? I don't have a rave kid boyfriend, and I've been doing it longer. I want one. Ted will do just fine. It isn't any fun going out with Juliana anymore, anyway. She gets really nervous whenever I want to do acid...and I still want to do acid all the time.

FIFTY-EIGHT

I go to Ted's small, dirty crap-box of a house in the worst town on Long Island. It's really far out east, before the Hamptons turn the land back to desirable. He gives me a hit of E. I almost never do that stuff, just because I'm not about to spend $25 for a questionable result when I can definitely be fucked up for a long time and 1/5 of the price on acid. Still, I'm not one to turn anything down. I do what I think you are supposed to do on ecstasy, and fuck him. He humps away on me and I guess I enjoy it? He showers me with lovely sentiments, a nice change even if they are often grammatically incorrect. We go into his backyard where he has a graffiti-covered shack that maybe used to be a child's playhouse. He rolls a big blunt and we smoke it. While we do, someone knocks on the door. They'd come to buy some weed. It's a good feeling, being the drug dealer's girlfriend. It's an admirable position, in its own way.

So, I am seeing three guys now: Darren; Chris, the pothead from CI; and Ted, the rave idiot. Each of them think they are the only one and none of them is enough. Luckily for me, Darren and Chris have no interest in parties, so my worlds spin on separate axes. Having run out of cohorts, I start going to parties with kids from my new high school. Cheyenne brings her friend Lana along, which is funny because we get her high and she's never even touched a cigarette before. That is so beyond my comprehension. We meet new friends, Lisette, Flora and Peter. They are Hispanic, black and gay, respectively, and between the three of them, they represent more diversity than I have ever been exposed to.

I am a little jealous because it was Cheyenne and Lana that had befriended them, really. They'd just started going out, for crying out loud. Now they are all tight with these new kids and I am on the outside, again. Fine, whatever, I am used to it there.

I don't understand what it is that makes me so "other." But apparently, it's pretty glaring. I go to hang out with this guy just because I know he has weed, and this other girl there whom I don't know – a girl who has a Puerto Rican accent, despite being a blonde chick from Long Island – questions my very humanity. I make some caustic joke while we sit smoking pot in this burnout's gigantic old Impala, and this pseudo-Latina girl in the back seat interjects, "You're weird, do you have fillings?"

I am shocked and open my mouth, pointing out the mass of mercury that fills my maw. "I do!" I exclaim, "does that make you weird?" I am thrilled to find the answer to all my awkwardness. Then she repeats, "No, FILLINGS, do you have FILLINGS." Oh. I finally put together that with her affected accent, fillings are FEELINGS. The realization reverberates within me. I seem like I don't have feelings? Me, who feels so overwhelmed by emotions all the time? It doesn't make sense to me. Clearly, I am putting out something entirely opposite to what I am feeling in.

FIFTY-NINE

And, speaking of putting out, hardy har har, I take my mom's car out to see Ted all the time, which infuriates her because she hates him. She thinks he's disgusting and she is right. He even annoys the fuck out of me. Ted is into smoking angel dust, which is not exactly the intoxicant of intellectuals. With him in my passenger seat, we pass a Plymouth Duster only to have him repeat the name of the car over and over and over again, laughing all the while. Right, Ted. Right. I get it. Still, I decide that I'd really love for him to come meet my father's family the next week on Christmas Day.

SIXTY

Christmas is going to be weird this year. It's the first one I've ever spent outside my childhood home. Some of my favorite memories growing up are sharing a bed with my sister on Christmas eve and waking up to find Santa-stuffed stockings hanging from her double bed posts. We'd run out in our pajamas and open all the presents from under our real Christmas tree. Carrie isn't going to come home for Christmas this year and we didn't get a tree. Mom is too mad at me, and the weekends that we could have gone to buy one I was either out clubbing or out cold. In the spot where our tree should be, she places a six-inch high decorative ceramic tree, with the faux-snow skirt around it to catch the needles that will never fall. It's really pathetic. She sure does know how to make a point. Every time I see that thing, I know it's my fault. She is clever, my mom, I have to give her that.

Darren joins me for Christmas Eve with my mother's family, the one where I play the role of sane, respectful daughter. Everyone likes Darren; he is a good guy. He can talk sports with my angry, athletic uncle, charmingly entertain my little cousins and listen intently to my grandfather's war stories. He got me so many presents too! A shirt and a bracelet and perfume. I feel kinda bad. I just get him some Eternity, perpetuating as I do a familiar odor for my lovers. I don't have a job after all. Everything I'd saved from the movie theater was gone, and I don't have anything to show for it. When I babysat and delivered papers, I had been able to buy so many tangible objects. Now I purchase nothing but memories, and blurry ones, at that.

I applied for a job at the nearby Blockbuster. They were really excited about it, what with my movie theater background. They even said they'd hire me at $5/hour instead of the usual $4.50. All they had to do is cut a little of my hair for a drug test and they'd call me with a schedule when they got the result. Once again, I don't flinch, but this is not something I could bluff through. The proof of my indiscretions was right there, in every follicle. Hell, they probably could've gotten high themselves, if they smoked it. I do not hear from them again.

Luckily, I am still able to retrieve some money from ye olde Bank of Locker Room, even with all the new school's security. It's a much riskier venture, if only because of the unfamiliar setting. This female security guard busted in on me once and asked what I was doing. I told her that I was using this bathroom because I had my period and was embarrassed. People do weird stuff like that all the time. She wasn't about to question me. I picked up over $100 that day, mostly from a little gift bag that had a sticky note which read "Freshman Field Trip Money" on it. It was so pathetic that I almost felt bad. What can I say? Kid should've locked it up. It's not even really my fault, when you think about it. I am teaching people a lesson. Stop being so stupid.

Between that coup and whatever Christmas money I get, I should be set for a little while. So, Darren goes home on Christmas Eve and I go out to Caffeine. They are having their annual "What the Fuck is Going On?" Christmas Party. They actually call it that. I go alone, but everyone I know is there. These are the die-hards. We aren't just doing this for fun. We'd spent all day with our families – it's our time now. In celebration of the holiday, they give out dipped cigarettes at the door, but I get there too late and don't get one. I don't even know what they are dipped in, but I don't care. I'm pissed that I missed the free mystery drugs.

There had been talk of getting me a cheap car for Christmas, but any hope of that diminished with every night that I didn't come home until morning. On Christmas Day, Dad has to come pick me up and bring me to my grandparents' house. He has been living there. Almost 50 years old and living with his parents. Fucking loser.

Christmas Day has always been spent with my paternal grandparents. First at their house in West Islip, with the inlet in the backyard that we could ice-skate on when it froze over. Grandma and Poppy would get a 15-foot tree for their atrium foyer, and the presents piled around it. There was a great old grandfather clock in the room where the fireplace roared, and Uncle Charlie played carols on the piano. It was the very image of holiday perfection. They had to sell that house and move into their summer house in the Hamptons when Poppy's record sleeve company went under. CD's were getting popular, see, but Poppy stuck with vinyl, convinced the discs were just a fad. Oops.

Poppy had been in business with dad's brother, Uncle Ned. Ned had a pretty blonde wife and three pretty blonde children. All of us having dark hair, with the exception of my father, we often felt like the photo-negative of their side of the family. My grandparents spent a lot more time with them, what with the shared business and all. I don't know if my dad was excluded from the family's company, or if he just didn't want any part of it. We felt the isolation though, in acts as insignificant as getting fewer presents around the Christmas tree. We were outsiders.

We will never be closer to our flaxen-haired family because my uncle and my father hate each other. Or, to be more precise, my uncle hates my father. I've never heard the reason, but it is pretty obvious just knowing what kind of person my father is.

Do I wish I was my uncle's child? No. Uncle Ned, while affable, clearly drinks to maintain his charm. One Christmas he made me downright ill. The kids were all watching the great sketch series "In Living Color," and he peered into the room and said, "They have their own show now?" He meant black people. Yeah, so he is gross. I confronted him about it at the time. Just another thing to drive a wedge between the two family factions.

Purportedly, my father's side of the family had been in the states forever…even included a President, Franklin Pierce. Sure, not a great President but a President, nonetheless. Mom says that my grandmother's father had been a banking giant, along the lines of Morgan or Stanley. This stuff is never spoken of. I guess I wouldn't speak of it either, since the family's illustriousness has clearly confined itself so firmly in the past. The men in my family seem to excel at bad business decisions. We are desiccated blue bloods, a family line grown crooked and broken. Still, they manage the pretense of propriety, while I fight against it at every turn, and bring the most disturbing of my suitors to meet them.

The Hamptons house is certainly no shame to behold, a pretty ranch with lots of land and a pool that even has a slide. After retrieving me from Hauppauge, Dad swings by Ted's and we arrive at the Christmas "celebration." Ted's cleaned up pretty well, but is still a slimy looking kid, with his bleached out hair and skinny little moustache. Plus, Ted was the name of my cousin's former long-term boyfriend that the whole family despised, so he is doomed by association. He gives me a tribal necklace though, which is so nice of him. They are supposed to look like they are made of bone, but most are wood and mine is plastic. I love it. I also love the ridiculously poetic greeting card, making far-too-early proclamations of love in grammar that verges on child-like. I appreciate these things as a collector would, not for any genuine reciprocity of emotion that I feel.

After dinner we go out for a cigarette, and Ted presents one that is slightly tinted. It's a leftover giveaway from the club the night before. Dipped in what, I don't know, liquid PCP? Does PCP come in liquid? I don't care what it is. It's there. It's Christmas. We're bored. Oh my god, we smoke it and its ass-smell of diesel fuel permeates the suburban cold. We go back inside and sit on the couch. We laugh and twitch. We zone out on the television. If anyone knows, they don't say anything. Maybe I always act as though I am on serious drugs, so it's hard to tell the difference. I don't really remember the rest of the night.

Ted comes with me to the mall the next day to return the crap that grandma had given me. She shops at Macy's, where you get cash back instead of store credits, even if you don't have a receipt. Generally, my grandmother is actually pretty good at shopping for clothes for her adolescent granddaughters, but she isn't versed in shopping for the counter-culture, nor, I'm sure does she have any desire to further my anti-feminine mystique. She is infuriated by denim itself, let alone my oversized versions of it. So, back to her favorite department store goes her matching sweater, turtleneck and leggings. As we wait in the long line, I pick up two more shirts and stuff them in my bag. When we arrive at the cashier, I am presenting twice the clothing I'd gotten, and am thusly given twice the cash. God, why is this stuff so easy?

SIXTY-ONE

School, however, is not proving as simple. I have to repeat the "Participation in Government" class. That's what my new school calls social studies...P.I.G. I am just beyond paying attention, beyond caring. I take economics and fail. It confuses me utterly. Between the numbers and the terms of art, I feel completely lost, and the moment I feel lost I don't try harder, I give up. That has always been my way. I still refuse to do any work outside of class, which would imply that I do any while I am in there. No...I have signed out. Unfortunately, I can't even get high anymore during the day to make it bearable. I take the risk once, right in the school's courtyard, trying to mask myself behind a bush. I take only two pulls when the security guard rolls up to take me to the principal.

"I don't know what it was like at your last school, miss."

I deny smoking weed, but admit to a cigarette. I say that I was having trouble adjusting and that I used to be able to smoke on campus. Hell, my last principal had bought the damn things for me. The security guard tells the principal that I had put the pot back into my wallet. Thanks a lot, killjoy.

"Let me see your wallet," the principal says. Sure, I reply, with my usual nonchalance. I toss it onto the desk. Once he finds the pot, he will certainly have me arrested. I've heard that they do that here. He looks through it, avoiding only the slot where he would find what he is looking for. My good fortune has prevailed once more. These people in power imagine that a guilty child will cave when challenged. I never back down, and they always give up their fight before I do.

The apartment is close enough to the high school that I can walk to and from there. I do so, and get high in both directions. Eventually, Chris – boyfriend number two - meets up with me after school, and I get high with him. Since I am still seeing and sleeping with Ted and Darren, I can take it slow with Chris and look like a pillar of modesty. My "chastity" makes it at least three weeks, which is pretty impressive for me. Once I start sleeping with Chris, I dump Ted. He is just too far away and too stupid to deal with anymore. Plus, the fact that I am seeing him upsets my mom so much and god knows I hate to do that. No, really, I do, in my own way. Upsetting her pulls heavily on my soul, just not as strongly as my desires do. Chris is just as bad a guy, maybe worse, but his baby face and aptitude for charm make him a more passable suitor for her daughter. I can still pass for a lively, effervescent and articulate young lady, after all. That is, when I'm not being a thieving, lying, drug-addled and slutty sociopath.

SIXTY-TWO

So varied are my extremes that, during the week, my mother almost forgets how angry she was the weekend before. As Friday approaches, she begs me not to go out. To just skip one weekend. But I can't do that. Who knows what I'd miss? The same thing happens every week, but I don't want to miss a minute of it. I might miss seeing English man, with whom I exchange occasional bon mots, but never fluids or phone numbers. By this time, I'd learned his name was Zack, and he isn't English at all, but Brooklyn Italian with a tongue ring that impairs his speech as much as whatever he is on each week. Somehow, all those verbal impediments rendered him a Brit in my eyes. I pursue him in my peripheral vision regardless of who has come out with me. Nothing ever happens between us, so it doesn't really matter if I lay some groundwork in the presence of a current lover, in hopes that Zack will be the future one. Sometimes our exchanges are limited to a head nod or sideways glance. It's torture. It's also highly possible he is the world's most ingenious rave promoter, inspiring a legion of young girls to follow him around to parties simply by tossing them a shred of hope.

I am so intent upon attending every event that I take my mother's car out in a blizzard. I really wanted to go to this new Friday night party, called The Living Room. Screw the snow, it's really fun there. I had to go. Zack had told me he would be there the next week, and some really good DJs were spinning.

Chris is the only one who is willing to come along for the ride as the snow swirls madly downward. By the time we get to the club, we learn via a note posted on the door that no DJs are coming, and that the music will be played from mix tapes. It really is that bad a storm. I feel like such a desperate asshole. Still, we hang around for a while and smoke a big bunch of weed before heading back home through the snow.

I love that the main thoroughfare on Long Island is the LIE. It stands for Long Island Expressway, but there is no end of amusement acknowledging that Long Island is built around a LIE. We're nearing home as Cammy's Camry hits a patch of ice and starts to slide. Chris yells "shit" as we revolve, seeing the lights of the oncoming cars as we continue to skid off the road, landing softly in the snow facing the opposite way that we had been traveling. The cars that had been right behind us shoot past as we gasp in mingled relief and disbelief. Five seconds later and one of those cars would have hit us as we spun. But we are okay. We are fine. I wait for the traffic to subside and pull back onto the road. The whole thing totally kills my buzz.

I return to Living Room the next week, this time with Lisette, Peter and Flora. Good thing, too. It would be awfully embarrassing to be seen with Chris, seeing as how he looks so much like Jason. See, Jason is here tonight. I don't even realize it until a pert, little blonde keeps walking by me, staring with wide eyes. My curiosity is piqued, as my own eyes are wide with acid. Just when I am about to ask what's up, she says, "Are you Jaime?" Her tone is devoid of meaning. I have no idea what this is about. I've been recognized. I feel like a celebrity. I admit who I am.

Her angelic little face contorts with rage as she puts it up toward mine, her hand raised with a flat palm like she might deal me a deathblow with her outstretched fingers. "If you EVER talk to Jason again, I will fucking KILL you." she spits. For someone who tends to have terrifying acid trips that involve my demise, I am strangely unfazed by this. Maybe because I am bigger than her, or because, for once, I am not guilty of whatever offense she's accusing me of. I have the right ammunition to retaliate. I haven't talked to Jason in months.

"Look," I say, "I don't know what he told you because he's a liar." With that, she brings back her hand into a fist, aimed at my face. I don't move. I don't flinch at all. I stare at her incredulously. What the fuck is she doing? I have to laugh. She puts her hand down. "Just stay the fuck away from him," she says before walking away. Lisette approaches me and asks what happened. I'm still not exactly sure. I am certain that I have won this time, though.

The rest of the night progresses just as weirdly, with superstar DJ Dmitri of Deee-lite spinning an off-kilter set that he pumps his fists at enthusiastically. In his large, brightly colored clothes he looks like a silly clown, and not the DJ god he is supposed to be. I meet a guy named Rocky who has his chin pierced and clearly garnered his sobriquet from the method of guttural, monosyllabic speech that he employs. We dance in the ridiculousness of it all. Then we smelled it, like burning baby diapers permeating the air. Everything slows down, seems serious. "What the hell IS that?" I ask the circle that I'm dancing with. "That's crack," Flora answers, portentously. Crack. Wow. Someone is smoking crack in this place. As wild as we are, there are lines you don't cross, and that is one of them. Who decides that smoking crack seems like a good idea? That just seems crazy. I laugh it off. "It's probably Jason's new girlfriend," I quip.

Something is happening with my dancing. I'm not as good anymore. I am filled with paranoia and fear. My fear of not being good enough makes me horrible. My once expansive, expressive moves have pulled back so that my feet do not lift, and my arms follow and repeat the same path over and over again. My friends start to make fun of me, and that makes it worse. "Look at Jaime dancing," they say, "what are you doing, why are you doing that?" I don't know. They are such good dancers. I'm not. I don't want to try. I don't want to look stupid.

It's not just with dancing either. We'll be chatting in a circle and when I go to interject, all the heads turn to me and I stutter and stammer. I forget what I'm about to say, or what I'm about to say seems too unimportant to have garnered all this attention, and I can't carry through. I go into the bathroom and stare into the mirror, falling into the holes that are my eyes. I am crumbling.

SIXTY-THREE

I finally get a job. It's at Contempo Casuals, a relatively cool clothing store in the mall, but I take three weeks to get them my working papers and they rescind their offer. I feel so stupid.

So, I'm forced to use a roll of coins to pay my club admission, and am met with the most derisive of glances. "You're kidding me," the doorman says. "What?" I reply, "it's money." He can't argue with that. The judgment kills me, but I'd had to make a choice: I know a drug dealer will not accept a coin roll.

Darren is getting angry that I don't hang out with him anymore. His new friend Brian started seeing Juliana and since they smoke pot, I'll hang out if they are going to be there, but otherwise hanging out with Darren means I'm not getting high. He takes me out for dinner though, that's nice. During appetizers at a horrible chain, my UTI hits me, a pervasive demon always seeking to rear its horny head. I know that I am doomed. I lose some urine as I race to the restroom. I tell him that I'd gotten my period and he gives me his coat to tie around my waist. He is a good guy. Better than I deserve.

Chris is more up my alley. We get high and screw, plus he lives only five minutes away. He doesn't have much to say and that does get to me. Plus, any attempt at argument with him is met with "whatever," but he likes me well enough. He throws rocks at my apartment window so that I can come meet him downstairs for our trysts.

Chris has this creepy older friend that I've heard lives in his car. Turns out he got some coke for all of us to share, so I guess he's not all bad. It's my first time trying it. I breathe it in quickly and send his friend away so Chris and I can get it on, because that's what I've heard you are supposed to do on coke.

Contrary to Sharon Stone's assertion in "Basic Instinct," it doesn't blow my mind.

SIXTY-FOUR

So, I finally get a job doing telemarketing for this insurance agent. Except for the repeated rejection from people, ranging from hang-ups to downright cruelty, it is a pretty sweet gig. I only have to get folks to answer questions about their car insurance and see if we can save them some money. People love saving money, so it isn't as hard as selling them something. I could never do that. Three nights a week, three hours a night, $10 an hour. Plus, if I hit my quota of 10 surveys, I can go home early. I am good at it, so Chris and his creepy car-living friend come and pick me up every night, get me high and bring me home. That's $90 a week. It's all I need.

I proceed to make friends with the more serious potheads at school. There is a group of younger, troublemaker boys that come back to my apartment and we get high and play video games before my mom gets home. It isn't a tawdry thing, I don't hook up with any of them. I am just one of the guys.

Mom comes home in a fury as she is met with our giggles and blaring red eyes. She tells me to get my friends out of there. "Fine," I say. I will just drive them home. "No, you won't," is her reply. I laugh, "stop me." I get to the door with my friends in tow. "See you in a minute," I say. "Yes, you will," she pointedly retorts. I don't pick up on her insinuation at the time, but I learn what it meant when I get to the car and see it fixed over the steering wheel… The Club, a locking metal device advertised on late night television, is there clamping the wheel, barring my passage. It is not the standard red, but yellow – it's The Economy Club, see - but it's still enough to put an end to my joy riding. I laugh. I have to hand it to my mom. That was a good one.

Chris steals car radios and says he can saw through The Club, but he can't. We hack away at it for a good twenty minutes before I feel too pathetic to continue. Looks like we'll have to find another way to get around.

It's probably good that I can't go out as much because I have my college auditions to think about. I am still planning on going to school for acting, but have obviously given up on Yale as an option. I've given up on most options, really. I don't want to think about it at all. Going to more school when I've already had such miserable experiences? No thanks. We have no money, but getting financial aid is going to be hard because we sold the house the year prior. It's funny, when I was in elementary school, I would pore through college guides, weighing my options. Now I can't be bothered, the concept pains me. I'd done fairly well on my SAT's, but it was the year there was an uproar because they changed it from an IQ-type test to something based in general knowledge, in which I certainly do not excel. I am definitely going to a state school; that much is clear. I want SUNY Purchase. They have an acting conservatory and take only 30 students out of 3000 applicants. It's also only 45 minutes north of the city. I set my sights on it and can't avert my eyes. That is what I want. I bother to apply for only one other school, SUNY New Paltz, another hour north, but New Paltz is more renowned for its hippie-party atmosphere than for its acting program. Lord knows that wouldn't suit me at all. Right.

The day before the Purchase audition, Chris gives me a ton of hickeys. He is always doing that, fucking dick. I am forced to wear a turtleneck. I walk in and my nerves buckle me. There is a heater clicking away in the corner and it distracts me. My comedic monologue gets a laugh, at least. I get home that night and go to Caffeine with the usual suspects, Lisette, Flora and Peter, plus Cheyenne and Lana can come along because it is a local thing. There is a promoter that we know whose name is Toast. You know, not his given name. They have all these promoters with stupid names: Toast, The Energizer Bunny, and Rhoda's ex, Slipshod Rob. That is an accomplishment, to get a name, I guess. I wish I had a name for myself. As we all dance, Toast sidles up to us holding some sort of canister that we are supposed to inhale from. I never ask what it is or what it will do. I just do it. He walks away and leaves me reeling, almost falling down and only righting myself by grabbing onto - apparently - Lisette's face. Oops, sorry. I am embarrassed. The stuff wears off quick, leaving a path of burnt synapses in its wake. I continue dancing in my self-conscious shame. What am I doing? I'd auditioned earlier that day for the school I really want to go to, and here I am all fucked up just hours later. What if they could see me now? I don't deserve to get in.

A week later, I have my New Paltz audition, which I rock because I don't care. I hadn't thought about it at all, it wasn't remotely important to me. They call the next day to let me know that they are calling all the actors who got high marks on their auditions to invite them to be a part of the program. That's a nice compliment. Can I call Purchase and tell them that New Paltz said that? Well, at least I have somewhere to go if Purchase doesn't come through. But it has to. It just has to. I want it so bad, there is no other option. I won't know for another month.

SIXTY-FIVE

Chris gets his friend to take us into the city. I don't care how I get in there, I just have to go. I've been talking to Rocky for a while, much to my mother's horror whenever she picks up the phone. I am going to meet Rocky at the club that night. I am letting one of my boyfriends drive me to meet this other guy. I have hit a new level of iniquity, and admit that I am a little nervous about it. How am I gonna handle this one?

We walk in and Rocky is standing right by the door. I awkwardly introduce everyone. We all go to the back room and smoke a joint to alleviate the tension that swims between us all. This is not to say that we would not have smoked the joint if there wasn't

any tension, of course. I have already dropped a hit or two of acid, and the pot is strong. We just keep smoking more. Rocky goes to the bathroom. "You told this guy to meet you here?" Chris asks with pain and confusion in his eyes. "Yeah,' I say, as a matter of fact. He is pissed but you almost can't argue with my detachedness. It must be infuriating.

I walk away to go to the bathroom. Rocky is standing there. He asks if Chris is my boyfriend and I admit that he is. One of them. I apologize coolly, but my head is swimming. Rocky turns angrily and walks out the door. I feel bad. Not so much guilty, but actually, physically bad. I start my walk back to Chris when the darkness washes over me. It starts at my feet, swims up and drags down. It envelopes my head, which smacks left side down against the concrete club floor. All those times that I pretended to pass out, and now it had actually happened. I lay there with my head spinning into the earth. It's spinning like the ball, like the light on the chain, and it is pulling me down. I am going to hell. I am certain that I am dying, and that I am going to hell.

A beatific, earth-mother woman swoops in and picks me up. "Are you okay?" I shake my head to indicate that I am. She asks if I've done acid and I say that I have. How does she know that? I wasn't aware that passing out was a common side effect of dosing. The angel sits me down. She says I'll be okay. In a few minutes I am as fine as she'd promised, but for a little while there, I had died.

SIXTY-SIX

Of course, I don't get into the SUNY Purchase acting program. I have been acting my whole life, how can they not see what is so clear to me? I guess that with my expulsion from acting school and my hickie-hiding turtleneck, I scream "liability" more than I do "potential." And hey, maybe I'm just not any fucking good. The school says that my academic record, remarkably, makes them interested in having me there as a non-thespian. Are they kidding me? This is not some great accomplishment, it's a state school and my average hovers in the upper 80's. Fuck that. They are wrong. I am an actor. But what if I'm not as talented as I've always convinced myself that I am? I had made Purchase the key to solving my life, the far-off utopia where I could make everything okay. Now what am I going to do? Whatever, I guess I'm going to go to New Paltz. They want me. Of course, like for most that want me, I have little regard in return.

I have to somehow finish up at Hauppauge High School first. They are having auditions for the spring play; that will get me through. It's "Marvin's Room," a play about cancer and a pretty bold choice for a high school, I'd say. This excites me. The director is Mr. Moulder and I'm in his acting class during the day. He seems to appreciate me. This should go just fine. Candy from a baby. There is the role of a dotty old grandmother, which is just my cup of Earl Grey.

Moulder has me read three times, howls emanating from the crowd all the while. Afterward, the kid who is the star of all the Hauppauge shows comes up to me, drops to his knees and bows to pay worship. How delightful! See? I'm right, I am good at this. Screw you, non-believers, I'll show you.

I'm also excited to be making a movie tonight for film class. I am partnered with Ryan, the pink-puffy-haired fella who has become my friend. He is doting and amorous, though effete. He oozes creativity. He makes zines and collages. He also makes me little gifts which he brings to me with loving respect in his eyes. Oh, Ryan is so lovely. He doesn't get fucked up though, so I don't have much use for him. Not to mention, I find both his pro-activity and his inexplicable regard for me wholly disconcerting. As a film class partner though, we are a perfect fit. I run the project like a totalitarian regime, with very little interest in the ideas of others. To see my zeal would be to almost believe that I care about school. This isn't like school, though, this is interesting. This is creative. It's so exciting! We've chosen to make a music video, or, rather, I have. We are going to use the first track from a Nasa rave tape that I have, a song called "Mr. Kirk." In it, the police come to a man's door and tell him that his son, age 17, has died of an overdose. It breaks into electronic beats littered with the repeated refrain of "overdose" and "your son is dead." That song freaks me out, for understandable reasons. It seems more of a challenge than a cautionary tale. That's the red flag we are going to make our video for, and we are going to do it at the local supermarket.

There is a picture of the supermarket manager in the entrance, and he becomes our Mr. Kirk. The shot starts on him and will flip through various angles of our in-aisle antics. It's late and the store is empty. Ryan, laying on a cart in the meat section, represents Mr. Kirk's dead son. I get pushed really fast in a cart down the aisle toward camera, and we pan through the section marked "drugs," an image made somewhat less impactful by the presence of Tums and Tylenol. Ryan holds a metal dog's leash and the camera follows it to where it is attached, my belly ring. We dance in the aisles and, in sync with a whip-like sound at the end of the song, I jump on a box of Life cereal, exploding its contents onto the floor. C'mon, we are 17 and therefore not ones for subtlety in our metaphors. We don't even clean it up. They've been so nice to let us shoot in here, and we just leave this big mess. We are exultant in our accomplishment, and I finish off some celebratory weed by myself.

SIXTY-SEVEN

It's the next morning, and I'm about to find out about the school play. Things are really looking up. A large crowd looms about the piece of paper that hangs outside the office wall. I walk up casually, prepared not to gloat. I look down the page. I look back up. My name isn't there. Excuse me? Nobody had done remotely what I had in that audition. Does he want the usual high-school caliber performances? Does he not want someone to stand out? I have to know. My face turns red as my head pounds and I fume. I storm to Mr. Moulder's classroom and burst in during his class, all the members of which turn toward me. I go right up to him and, with quiet intensity declare, "I demand an explanation." He scoffs, "Are you kidding me?"

Everything goes black with rage, I don't know how I reply. I don't know how I leave the room. Did I say that there was no way I wasn't the best person for that part? Did I turn and skulk out, having been shamed by my boldness? I don't know. I had passed into another world. I guess it's a good thing that I didn't kill him. I hear it's during such blind furies that these things happen. When I return to myself, I am tearing around the courtyard, asking anyone if they have any weed. I had finished mine last night, fucking idiot. I need some now. Need it. Nobody is holding. I go straight home. Fuck the rest of the day. Fuck this school. I go home and cry, scream and cry like I hadn't in so long. Not getting my way seems like a curse.

Whatever, I am going to Lisette's later. I'll get fucked up there.

SIXTY-EIGHT

Lisette is from CI, the same town as Chris. Her family has a large house in a cul de sac, and though that gives the air of pleasantness in description, it is, in actuality, rather downtrodden. The house is dark and in disrepair. Her mother pads about in a bathrobe and speaks to us in broken English. Lisette has a 5-year-old brother, and another brother who is just a year younger than us who is a graffiti writer. He is known as Goose, like his tag. He is out for the night, but we hang out in his room. A red siren light swirls and each wall is covered in spray-painted scrawls. In their house. How do their parents allow this in their house?

There are a few of us hanging out, getting high. Then Johnny shows up. I've seen him around raves before, they call him Johnny Hands because he is a great dancer. He does "liquid dancing," moving his hands as though around an orb. He is truly a marvel to watch. As he walks in, everything slows down. We take each other in. The left side of his face is a huge crimson scab. There are murmurings that there had been a fight, but we don't talk about it. "Something went down," he says. "Looks like you did," I reply, holding his gaze. I knew, I had gone down too. Last weekend at the club, the left side of my face hitting the floor and grinding right in. It looked to me like Johnny had gone further down.

So, here he is, laying low at Lisette's. Apparently, he is detoxing from heroin. Heroin. I have never been around heroin. Sure, people say there can be some found in ecstasy, but that seems negligible. Heroin holds no allure for me. Like crack, it signifies too far a transgression. It carries death with it. I feel close enough to that as it is.

The people peel off to go home or to bed until there is just Lisette, Johnny and I curled up on Goose's bed. Johnny breaks out a white powder that he divides into three portions on a CD case. He says it is crushed up ecstasy. Maybe it is. It could be anything, it doesn't matter, I would do it either way.

Our already altered states expand. Everything softens but our awareness is keen. As we talk, it becomes very clear that something is lying heavily in the air. Something between Johnny and I. It isn't sexual it's...more than that. He is hearing me, the things that I say. They mean something to him. He is hearing them on a level beyond the superficial. He hears every wave in the undercurrent of my thoughts. Our eyes keep connecting. Lisette is starting to get tired and probably uncomfortable. She tells us she is going to bed. Do I want to go with her? No. Am I sure? Yes. Johnny and I look at each other. We need to talk. We have something to say to each other. We communicate this without articulating it. Lisette is concerned, curious. She leaves us alone in Goose's room.

The second Lisette exits, Johnny and I stare at each other, brimming with possibility. We talk excitedly about going to parties. I start to tell him about my experiences, that something is going on, that I've been doing strange things and nobody would acknowledge it. He stops me. He says he knows. He'd been there each time. That first time, at Essence, he'd been the one to trace his flashlight on the path of my spinning ball. He saw the scratching on the big projected record. He's seen everything, he says, it wasn't in my mind. All of it was real.

It is such a relief. I've felt like I was going crazy all this time, all of it building up inside me with nobody to listen and understand. Every time I'd brought it up it had been dismissed uncomfortably, which made me suspicious. "Other people can't handle it," Johnny said, "they don't get it. They don't live their lives on the level we do. We are tapped into something."

"But something bad is going to happen," I sputter, "isn't it?" He agrees that it is. The world is coming to an end. "But we're going to make it, aren't we?" I ask. Johnny nods with tears in his eyes. We hug so tightly and our mingled souls soar up to the sky. We are going to be okay.

I have my notebook with me and show him my doodles, mere scribbling that we look at as topographical maps of my psyche, likely of great import. We talk like that until the morning and go downstairs to the kitchen for some cereal. I manage a little, but I'm not really hungry.

I sit on the living room sofa with Lisette's 5-year-old brother, watching cartoons. All of the cartoons seem very serious. The characters all manipulating each other, trying to kill each other. "Do you see this?" I ask the little boy, "What do you think of this?" He puts his hand down on my chest. "Your heart," he says, "your heart." I look into his tiny face, which is pleading with me so earnestly. I become filled with my customary fear of demise. "What do you mean about my heart?" I ask him. He just repeats, "Your heart, your heart." I go back upstairs. That kid was really freaking me out.

Everyone starts coming over to Lisette's, getting ready to go out to a party that night. I had planned on going before but now...I've been in the same clothes since yesterday and I haven't showered, but beyond that, I don't want to go to a party. I don't want to be with all of these people that don't understand. I want to stay with Johnny. I need to talk to Johnny more, and he wants to introduce me to some of his friends. Friends that understand things on this level we are operating on, he says.

Lisette, Flora and Peter go out to the party and Johnny's friends skulk into the room with Goose, Johnny and me. They are a coalition of the type of folks most people would walk across the street to avoid. They huddle across the room as Johnny and I hold court from Goose's bed. He needs me to be touching him, because whenever I'm not, he is wracked by the pains of withdrawal.

"So, you guys hookin' up?' one of the kids asks sardonically. Everything that is said seems barbed and base. I tell them that we aren't, it is something more than that between us. "Right," they laugh. "Why aren't you hooking up?" We look at each other, I don't know why. After everything we'd just shared, it would make sense. We kiss deeply. A murmur goes up from the room. "Oh, shit' someone says. "Beauty and the beast," another interjects.

They are contrarians. For every positive thing that I say they have a negative counter. Every word is a euphemism, and the options roll around the room. A bowl isn't just for cereal. It is a pipe for smoking, a place for shitting. Everything is boiled down to its elemental basis: shitting, fucking and drugs. I don't know why Johnny wanted me to meet them. I don't like them at all. If I have come to a new place of consciousness, it is with a wide-eyed optimism, not their diseased and contorted misanthropy. They finally leave around the time that Lisette and Peter come back from the rave. They are still tripping, still dancing. Peter is bugging hard, dancing in front of a standing fan. I tell him that it is going to be okay. He doesn't have to get fucked up anymore, none of us do. We don't need that. A whole new world of opportunity and lightness is opening up before us.

Every time that I turn away from Johnny, pay attention to anyone else, I turn back to find him clawing at himself, and writhing in pain. It is a big responsibility. I haven't done drugs since that one line late Friday night, but I also haven't slept, eaten or showered since then. It's Sunday morning.

Out of nowhere, in the middle of this graffiti-covered room, its siren light still spinning, the techno music stops and a Morrissey song comes on. My favorite solo Morrissey song, a B-side, "The Girl Least Likely To." Oh my God, it is for me.

Where did it come from? It has to be for me. I sing along at the top of my voice, "Somebody's got to make it, she screams, so why, why can't it be me?" I get up and I dance, free and filled with love and infinite understanding. I am one with the universe. All is well, all is beautiful.

The techno music returns, and within it I begin to hear a repeated exhortation in a rapid staccato, "Call your mom, call your mom. Call your mom, call your mom." That's weird. I do what it says.

My mother picks up the phone, frantic. "Where are you?" It doesn't occur to me that she hasn't heard from me all weekend, and I don't understand why she is so upset. Everything is really fine, it's actually wonderful. "I'm at Lisette's," I answer. "I'm coming to get you," she says, before hanging up the phone.

When I was a little girl and my mother said that to me playfully, I would scream and run into her arms. I hate the idea of being chased. I am glad that she is coming to get me now. I love my mom. I look forward to running into her arms.

I trot down to her car, my eyes half the size of my face, which is drawn with dehydration and malnourishment. I am wearing the same fleece pullover and baggy jeans I left the house in on Friday morning. I reek. The fact that she didn't know where I was all weekend doesn't faze me. "It's okay, mom," I tell her, with a Puerto Rican accent, "I understand everything now." I'd talked to Johnny for so long that I now sounded like him.

Mom brings me back to the apartment. A newspaper sits on the kitchen table, its cover shot a glaring emblem of my new understanding. Everything is coming to a head. It makes perfect sense. I show it to mom.

The picture is from Washington Square Park in Manhattan, where I have been many times. There is a large cobblestone circle, rimmed by a metal fence. A police car sits idle on the far side of the circle. The center is empty, but opposite the police car, closest to the camera, a tree reaches up to the sky. Next to it, a man lays splayed on the ground, dead. The paper describes it as a classic case of murder-suicide. I know why he did it, I explain to my mother. "You see? She was at the center of the circle and he couldn't reach her." The tree stretches to heaven next to where he had fallen, doomed to the outer circumference of this circle of life.

Mom calls my therapist. We are going to see her in an hour. I am fine with that, I am fine with everything. The doorbell rings. It is the Newsday delivery person, seeking to collect his due. He has been trying for weeks, apparently. "This is not a good time' my mother tells him, shutting the door. "No mom," I exclaim emphatically, "you must pay the Newsday man!" How can she think of doing anything else, seeing the truth he delivers? I am insistent. She quickly throws money at him to make him go away.

We drive to my doctor, the day more vivid than I have ever seen. I still haven't changed or showered. I get there and tell her that I have it all figured out. I'm not going to do drugs anymore, but this has nothing to do with drugs. Something is happening in the world, something serious and dire, and I am a part of it. My therapist talks to me for no more than five minutes before she puts in a call to the hospital. She calls South Oaks, and they are ready to take me back.

The dead-souled woman in the intake office types away on her keyboard. Beeps occasionally emanate from her machine. I get up to dance to the music that it's creating. There is music in everything. The world is giving me messages all the time. They shepherd me upstairs, back to the ward I'd left just two years before. I start to notice that the doctors, all men, speak with cruel and detached derision. Their demeanors leave me at sea, where I am then rescued by kindly lady nurses, empathizing with their eyes. Why do they understand? The men do not understand, they just hurt me more. The men have always hurt me more.

Their physical exam uncovers my belly button ring. I look down at it as though I had been unwittingly tagged by researchers. The doctors are going to remove it. "Yes," I say, "take it out." The ring has now become an emblem of the damage I've done to my body, pouring forth it's poison from my middle. "Get it out! Get it OUT!" I scream.

You need some food, they say. Food. Yes, I do. I need food. We all need food. They place me at a small table by the entrance to the ward, overlooking the roomful of fellow inmates all eating dinner. Dinner. I haven't eaten in three days. They put a tray in front of me with roast chicken, rice and green beans. The sight, the smell of it makes me sick. I can barely open my mouth. I have no saliva. Chewing has become an alien activity to be relearned. The room buzzes around me and I raise my head to see that I've become the main attraction in the human zoo. A lean, elfin boy who doesn't seem older than 13 leans forward at his table and waves to me. I laugh and tears spring to my eyes as I wave back, returning the signal that had been sent to me. The boy rises from his seat and starts to approach. I lean forward in anticipation of the event to follow when a nurse lifts my tray.

"Come on," she says, "you're not staying here." I am obedient. I do not question the world as it presents itself to me. I follow her down an ever-elongating hall through the locked doors that require the use of her security card to open. We walk through a ward where more young people collect to herald my coming, only to be whisked past them to another set of doors.

We enter a darkened room. A TV flickers in the corner, a man dying on the screen. It looks like Goose, Lisette's brother

Goose. Goose is dying. I hear a loud whirring noise, a charging, chugging noise that starts slowly and grows, banging away. It sounds like a train. Goose is getting on the train. His train is leaving the station. There is a tapping, a rhythmic rap on the wall. Someone is trying to contact me. I go to the noise and tap my response via fingertip, _ _ .. _ _ _/_ _ .._ . _ _ . It is my code, the code that has been drummed into me. The noise subsides. Goose's train has left. I tell them, the staff and patients, that Goose is dead. I had heard it and seen it.

The other patients all look like warped versions of people I already know, and they stare at me in wonder. The nurse tells me that the noise I'd heard was just the washing machine in the next room. I say okay, but I'm not sure.

They sit me down with my food again, and I try to eat it. The fork is too heavy to lift to my mouth as I slide off a piece of chicken between my dry lips. I open and close my jaw. That's how you chew. Flavors shoot out like poison to the barren landscape of my mouth. I inhale through my nose to facilitate swallowing. I move my tongue and head back, like a baby bird. It is hard to get anything down. I don't manage much.

My mom has dropped off a bag of clothes. I didn't get to see her, but there, in the office, my clothes have appeared. I am so grateful. I strip off my rancid ensemble. They ask what I want done with them. "Burn them," I say. They are poisoned. I go into the shower to wash myself and the water is a rebirth. A big Black nurse sits right outside the open shower door. Not looking at me, exactly, but watching. Making sure I don't do something. What would I do? Slip down the drain, maybe. They have taken away my shoelaces too, as if I might kill myself. I had almost done that so many times before, but I don't want to now. I feel so good. I am on this earth for a reason. I get it now.

She watches, too, as I use the bathroom. She tells me to

try and go, though I don't have to. I'm not ashamed, it's just business. It's what is happening. She has to check what I'd come out with before I flush. There is almost nothing, urine and some small pellets of shit. I hadn't crapped in days either and I know that's bad. I have been full of shit, and now it is time to clear it all out. Nothing is crass in these circumstances. There are times in life when shit, as much as people don't want to talk about it, is the most important thing there is.

"Looks like a rabbit's been here," she says. Immediately I think of that rave promoter, the Energizer Rabbit. I gasp. She is right, I tell her. A rabbit has been here. I put on the fresh, clean pajamas my mother brought me. They are cotton heaven. I lay down in bed and tried to sleep for the first time in almost 72 hours. The door is left open. Out in the hall, the nurse has set up a small table with a red light, almost like the red siren I'd been transfixed by for the whole weekend. She would spend the entire night like that, outside my door with the red light. It makes me anxious as I try to drift off.

I don't know if I've slept when I hear the guy's voice in the hall. I had maybe slept a weird non-sleep, where time passes but you feel like nothing's changed. I see his longhaired shadow play in the red hall light. He is asking the nurse if she's seen Mary Jane. He is looking for Mary Jane. The nurse sends him off, back to his room. There is no Mary Jane here, she asserts. I lay in bed and his words race through me. I am impelled toward the hallway nurse, ominous in the dark with her light. I am certain though, and I have to let her know. "He's looking for me," I tell her.

"He's looking for Mary Jane," she says. "I know," says I. "But you're Jaime," she glares at me. "But I think I might be Mary Jane." I've smoked so much pot, see. Mary Jane is whom I represent, in a larger, more cosmic ethos. He must be looking for me. I must be Mary Jane. She sends me back to bed.

When I meet him the next day, I am disappointed. I thought perhaps we had some lesson to learn from one another but he is devoid of lessons, of life. His name is Justin. That said it right there, he was just in. Brand new. He is gone by the end of the day, probably to a ward for the lucid. He's left the state that brought him here. I don't realize it, but "here" is "flight deck." The mythologized marvel I'd heretofore only imagined. I've done it. I've taken off. I am in the clouds.

I am tested for cognitive functioning. I have to read aloud a list of words that increase in difficulty toward the end of the page. I read them with similarly increasing speed, trying to quickly unlock the code that has been set before me. I finish the list and look up expectantly. They don't tell me what my accomplishment means, but I have proven that my brain, though turned to mush, is at least a high-functioning sort of mush.

A nurse sits by the door, taking notes as I talk with the other patients. I talk incessantly, stringing each thought together like trapeze artists in a never-ending routine. We eat cereal from our bowls and we go from bowls to bowls and forks to fucks and instead of getting a trophy we atrophy and we all talk too much we talk too much we talk too much. My body joins in the flow that my torrent of words is creating. My hands swirl in ever-tightening circles.

"Three strikes and you're out," the nurse says. Whether it is her implication or not, I assume that she is speaking about me. In this place. I've been in this hospital twice now. A third time will rule me out. Out of society. Out of my mind. You can't go to a mental hospital three times and be okay, for Christ's sake.

I want to be okay. I don't want to do drugs anymore. I take a small juice box from the ward's refrigerator and ask the nurses what ascorbic acid is. I don't want the acid. I had done quite enough acid, thank you very much. She assures me that it is just a preservative for the juice, and that it is okay for me to have. I am uncertain. The nurse goes so far as to get the dictionary to look up "ascorbic acid" with me. I hesitantly acquiesce. I have to draw the line somewhere though. We go outside after a storm for a cigarette. I sip on a cup of tea in the cold dampness. A drop of rain falls from a tree branch overhead and into my cup. I put the cup down. When the nurse asks why I've abandoned my beverage, I tell her, with utmost seriousness, "acid rain."

I can't sleep at night. Wired, wired, wired. I go out to the nurse's station. The guy on duty shows me the bags of clothing brought in by the other patient's parents. The first bag is marked with the letters JJ. "Jen Johnson," I say, referring to the girl in my school who had been in that catalogue. Seems I am always hallucinating about her. I think her initials on that bag are an indication of her death.

Everything I see is a sign of something bad. He holds up the clothes in the bag, one piece at a time, and I ruminate about each. He takes out an oversized t-shirt with the Looney Toons characters on it. But these Looney Toons characters have been given an urban face-lift, in a current, horrifically misguided trend. Bugs Bunny wears baggy jeans and a backwards cap. He is jumping in the air and screaming off to the side of the shirt. I look at it in wonder. "That's what's wrong with everything," I say. "The Looney Toons used to be so innocent. Now they're trying to be cool and they are losing themselves entirely."

SIXTY-NINE

My mom and dad come to visit. There isn't a special room or area in flight deck, they just come right onto the ward and sit with me on a couch outside the nurse's station. Dad meets my wild-eyed stare with something like understanding. It's confusing. He gets me now?

I rant to them about the state of the world, how I have figured it out, how we are all just trying to connect and some people want to turn off the connections and that's why we can't cum. I actually say that to my mother. I don't have any reason to think my mother has any trouble climaxing, but in that moment, I am sure she does, and that I know why. They've been loading me up with Halydol, an anti-psychotic. That's what I am now, apparently: psychotic. I wouldn't believe them if they told me that, not as clearly as I am seeing the world. My parents get up to leave. As the thick doors closed behind them, my mother falls to her knees and weeps. I am gone, and there is no indication that I am ever coming back.

They say that only crazy people think that they are sane. So why isn't it possible that psychotics are the ones who have it right? I certainly feel different and stronger with my newfound viewpoint. I'm not interested in drugs anymore, likely because I still haven't come down from the last ones, but still…I call Chris and dump him. He says he will quit smoking pot for me but I know he can't. He *is* pot. Then I call Darren, the "good" boyfriend, in an attempt to rebuild what I'd done my best to destroy. I am just going to be perfectly honest. If I believe in anything now, it is the truth. I tell him that I am in the hospital, but I am okay. I'm really great, actually, and I'm going to be really great to him from now on.

He is quiet for a while and then he tells me. His best friend Brian had shot himself. Brian is dead. It makes perfect sense to me. I knew it, I say. Something had shifted, and everyone is dying. People can't take the world the way it is. He is not comforted by my words. He asks if I'd heard that Kurt Cobain had killed himself too. I hadn't. My blood drains to my feet. The lead singer of Nirvana, the voice of our generation's malcontent, is dead too. It had all happened in these last few days, and I had felt it all. Something real had happened, was happening. Darren says he doesn't want to see me anymore.

SEVENTY

I am being moved off flight deck. Through the doors I go with my shopping bag of belongings. This is the adolescent substance abuse unit. I am given a room with a butch older girl who had been binge drinking. There are about 20 kids in various stages of pot, coke or dope-headedness. Unlike the kids on flight deck, these patients can formulate sentences and have far lower (though not completely absent) incidences of screaming, crying, or self-abuse. They took me off of flight deck because my roommate there stole some cleaning fluid and I had to stop her from drinking it. I guess the fact that I hadn't joined her for a swig was reason enough to have my condition downgraded. I'd been on flight deck for a week.

The kids on the ward call me mom as I gasp in horror at their persistent desire to use. I feel so beyond that now. They just want to get fucked up. I maintain that the world is fucked up enough, and joining it is just the easy way out. They laugh at me. They make me dance for them. I am always glad to dance. I can do it again.

One kid on the ward, Tito, is a thug who'd been kidnapped when he was 4. He was returned to his mother ten years later to little more reception than, "Oh, you're back." Another guy, Sean, has been in treatment centers since he started using at 12. He is trying to kick heroin now. God, he is beautiful. He won't talk to me, though, won't even look me in the eye. Before he is discharged, I ask him why he is so mean to me. He admits it is because he is jealous. He is jealous that I am so sure that I won't use again, because he can't be that sure. He wants to stop though, most kids there don't. They are there by court order or parental influence. The day he gets out, Tito calls us three hours later to say he is driving down Queens Boulevard with an 8-ball of coke. "See ya, suckers," he says. I feel so sorry for him. I feel sorry for all of them. Maybe it is easier for me to look forward to a future, with my aspirations and comparatively pleasant life circumstances. For others the fight will be harder, because most of them have so little to fight for.

We have Narcotics Anonymous meetings on the ward, with guest speakers sharing their stories of woe. I relate to these people. They had seen the dark side and stepped into the light. I will be like them. They give me a program to follow when I get out. A list of meetings, a book of the 12 steps. I am going to be released the next day. Once again, I'm not so sure that I am ready for the world, but my mom's insurance disagrees. I figure that I might as well be discharged; I haven't ever felt ready for the world and another few days isn't going to change that.

A neurologist comes in to test me before I leave. Touch my fingertips to my nose, follow the point of his pen with my eyes, bend down to my toes and come up again. He sighs with exasperation. "You're completely fine." He says it like he is angry that I haven't come away with some synaptic scar, a brain-bent-badge of my self-abuse, or a signpost of warning to all who dared dabble as I had. Just lucky, I guess.

I find out that Johnny had tried to get admitted to the hospital with me. Had stood outside its windows waiting for me to look out. But I never did. And I never did see him again. But sometimes I suspect that, if the world should experience the cataclysm we spoke of in that graffiti-covered room, that the smoke will clear and I'll see Johnny there, dancing.

SEVENTY-ONE

Dad is picking me up from the hospital because mom has to work. I stare out the passenger window of his car as we travel north on route 110. A disheveled man walks on the side of the road. I dub him a user. I can see it. I can still see everything so clearly. People's spirits shine out through their skin and write truths in the space around them.

I am tense, but then, I am always tense around dad. He is quiet, and a deep swell of anger starts to boil inside of me. We drive through the Roy Rogers for some fried chicken and biscuits. I snap my order at him. His lack of reassurance, his inability to communicate with me, is infuriating.

"Why do I have all this anger? Why do I hate you so much? What did you do to me?" I scream, crying. I want the truth, I want nothing but the truth. He is shaken. He says he didn't do anything. He does call me a few hours later, though, to suggest a neighbor that might have done something to me, abused me in some way. Do I remember the guy? From two doors down? No. No, I don't.

SEVENTY-TWO

My friends won't talk to me, Juliana, Gina. I speak to them like a missionary to heathens. I tell Juliana that I am sorry about Brian, but that we are all heading down that road and it should be a lesson. She isn't interested. She does tell me that the raver Super Dave had died as well. Gina tells me this chick Peanut is gone too. The toll mounts. What sort of cosmic sweep had occurred? Super Dave and Peanut...they had relinquished their names and their selves, and now their lives.

But I still have Ryan. Sweet, puffy-haired, sober Ryan. He comes by the apartment with a wood box he'd made for me. The inside is lined with sand and shells. Normally, I'd put my varied paraphernalia inside of a box like this. Now what do I put in there?

I am glad that Ryan can be my friend now that drugs won't distract me from him. He also brings me a military-style metal box, and in there, I decide, will go my memories of the sordid life I had lived: rave flyers and love letters from druggy losers. I am 17 and putting my past behind me. He shows me the video we'd made at the supermarket the night before I'd gone crazy. It seems so eerily prescient. He'd edited it perfectly. We had gotten an A.

When I return to school, I have another project to do, this time on my own. I do another music video to another rave song. It opens with a symphony which snaps into rapid break beats as a picture of the earth gives way to one of a mushroom cloud, and I narrate a poem about the recent reclamation of my self. I literally put a piece of paper marked "SELF" inside the wooden shell-filled box that Ryan gave me. "Things are always better from the outside don't look in; things are better from the outside just don't bother looking in..." Clearly, I retain the more heavy-handed aspects of my insanity.

My classes have become a platform for my new worldview. For a Creative Writing assignment, in which we have to write a poem using a singular rhyme scheme, I write this:

They made him known as Super Dave,
Was always seen at every rave,
Polo gear and drugs he'd crave,
It took him to an early grave.

Mr. Gethmart, my creative writing teacher asks about it. It turns out he is the father of this guy Ralph, a friend of Eryn's with whom we had gone to parties. Ralph had moved on from ours to an even faster crowd. I write about nothing but my experience of the last months, and to hear so vividly of the circles that his son and I had been revolving in must make him concerned. Mr. Gethmart is a sweet man, and to look at him now makes me cry. So I tell him that I am worried Ralph has a serious drug problem. Oops. I have never been one for repression, but my newfound clarity is a truth serum.

My obsession with death persists, as evidenced by the final project of our film class. Ryan and I partner again, with Cheyenne this time. Once again, I choose the song: The Smiths' "Pretty Girls Make Graves." Ryan is so fey, he is perfectly suited for the role of the singer, lamenting his inability to love a girl. It really is remarkable casting. We frolic upon a rocky North Shore beach. A shot that starts on pretty, feminine legs in the water pans up to reveal a dress containing a lip sync-ing Ryan. He looks so lovely. Cheyenne and I are the taunting, titular pretty girls. The video closes with Ryan spinning lazily on a playground toy. It really is beautiful. I am so proud. I love making things. I love that people like the things I make. I just wish that I could do that all the time.

Unfortunately, though, there are other subjects to contend with, and in each of them, I am completely overwhelmed and failing.

I am signed up for this after school, outpatient treatment facility, the idea being that I should not be left to my own devices in the hours between school and my mom coming home. Apparently, this is an adolescent's "prime using time." I hate that I have been so identifiably part of a larger societal pattern. Every day, I wait for the minivan to pick up myself and four other miscreants, each in varied states of degradation. One kid doesn't even use drugs so much as he is totally strange. We have therapy and art projects, it's like a crazy-kid nursery school.

Toward the end of the program, our parents are invited for a session. The subject comes to acid, a subject on which I consider myself quite the expert. I've heard somewhere that, in the eyes of the law, you can legally be deemed insane if you've taken more than seven hits of acid in your life. I suggest this as a guideline for responsible usage, knowing that I, personally, have far surpassed the limit several times over. The logic infuriates someone's father and he starts screaming about where I've come up with this "magic number." Were I a more hurtful person, I would tell him that, with his irrational anger, I now saw the genesis of his child's problems. As it is, however, I cry and storm out. Two other girls have already done just that. This is not a group conducive to constructive conversation.

SEVENTY-THREE

I lost my job while I was hospitalized, so I have no more money coming in. Of course, without drugs, I don't need to spend much money any more. Now that my mother approves of my social life, she can safely dole out small sums on which I can go to dinner or clubs. Yes, to clubs, she still lets me go. I go with Ryan now; straightedge Ryan is as innocuous as a gerbil. Not only has he never done a drug, he's never even kissed anyone. He is like the inverse of me. I've done enough for the both of us. He can be socially awkward, which is annoying, but my other friends don't want to go out with me. I don't blame them. However I may try to appear laid back and fun, the fact of my hospitalization and consequent abstinence must be a persistent anathema to their good time.

Ryan and I drive to rave at a warehouse in Queens. As I walk in, I see that promoter the Energizer Rabbit. I nearly spew to him the story of how, in my darkest moment, he'd been tangentially ascribed responsibility for my constipation. Thankfully, I manage to wrangle some rare repression. He stands at the door like a roadblock to my sobriety. He asks how I am doing and I tell him I am clean. He laughs and says we'll see how long that lasts. I'll show him.

Parties definitely aren't as fun without drugs. It's funny how dancing for several hours isn't nearly as easy without their effects. According to Narcotics Anonymous, I shouldn't be putting myself in these situations. I am going to meetings as another stipulation of my release from the hospital. The meetings are filled with haggard older folks, chain smoking and drinking coffee in church basements and community centers. They tell thrilling stories of abuse that far outweigh my own. Most of them don't talk to me. Bright eyed and cheery, still loopy from the effects of my psychosis, I feel like a joke to them. I'd been a pothead for god's sake. I hadn't whored myself or tried to smoke whatever was white that I'd found on the floor. I live at home with my mother. I am in high school. I am 17, for crying out loud. What do I know from suffering?

There is a place for me in this world, however. On Wednesday nights in Port Jefferson, there is a youth meeting. I look at this, not just as a joining of like-minded peers, but as a phenomenal dating opportunity. Sure, NA says you shouldn't date for the first year of your sobriety, but I have to maintain at least one of my vices. Without drugs or men, who would I be? What would I do?

I go outside for a smoke after the meeting and there he is: Rhoda's ex-boyfriend Tom Sparks, the one that had robbed her. He is out of rehab and has to go to meetings too. It turns out that he lives in Hauppauge. He had even gone to and been kicked out of the same school that I am going to – and could be kicked out of – now. What a small, small world. He is still hot. Rhoda had been with my ex already, it's not like we have any allegiance there. Tom and I start going out right away. His treatment program has to meet with me, to establish whether or not I am a suitable partner for their charge. With just over a month clean, it is decided that I am not. We imagine ourselves a modern-day Romeo and Juliet, and whine to each other in choked voices about the lack of fairness of it all.

Our parents have to acquiesce in some way. After all that had transpired with their children, simply dating seems an innocent enough venture. I am allowed to go to Tom's house some nights. We listen to music and fool around. I try to hold out, to really build a relationship before sleeping with him. I last maybe a week and a half. Our time is so limited and the stakes seem so high, making love is a necessary dramatic step. Mazzy Star's "Fade Into You" is involved. It is solemn. It is lovely.

Or, well, it would be if I wasn't still sleeping with Darren. We aren't going out anymore, but we still hang out and get it on. The funniest part about it is, I am so hurt that Darren no longer wishes to be committed to me, even though I had never been faithful to him. I am equally fretful about Tom's fidelity, despite my very current lack of it. I am a hypocrite, but I don't realize that. It is more like I am actually several separate and wholly divergent people. I am just an endless hole of need, seeking to be filled however possible. The drugs are gone, and I am just replacing them with the intoxications of the opposite sex.

Darren wants to try loving in an alternative orifice and I give it to him. I cry and I tell him that I love him. He tells me that he feels bad. I do too, and not the least bit fulfilled. What am I looking for? What do I need? Cheyenne and I hang out with Darren and acid-giving Andy the next week. We smoke cigarettes while they shoot basketballs at a curbside hoop. Darren says his job delivering TVs for a chain store is a pain in his ass. "Your ass!" I scoff. Cheyenne and I giggle knowingly, like the trashy little girls we are.

SEVENTY-FOUR

Cheyenne and Lana come with Ryan and I to Caffeine. It is awkward to be there whilst fully alert, and totally cognizant of my every awkwardness. The girls still take drugs. It makes me mad, and makes them rise quickly through the ranks of the raver social circles. I am a footnote, a sidebar. The straight girl nobody really wants to talk to, lest they be led to believe that whatever they are doing might be wrong. And I do think they are wrong. I still feel elevated. I don't need drugs.

I am worried about this house party though. It's being held by Ramon, the boy voted "cutest" at school. He is a surfer/stoner guy with whom I have shared a mounting flirtation in the face of his recent dumping at the hands of his so-hot-it-is-forgivable-that-she-is-a-sophomore girlfriend. The day of the party he comes up to me, high and lacking affect to say, "Some China men have big dicks." Okay. I am flummoxed by this, seeing as how he isn't Chinese and presumably not gay. I take it as a flirtation, and thusly counter that some girls who ride horses make good lovers. There is no subtlety in that. Such a fine young lady.

Everyone stumbles around Ramon's backyard. Red cups of beer and the smell of marijuana are everywhere. Oh, my sweet friend Mary Jane, she smells so good. Still, there is some satisfaction in my abstinence. I feel an exaltation that almost - almost - overtakes the tension. The need. The need that is always there, urging me, forcing me to do something, anything to get outside of myself. I grab Ramon, only shades above consciousness, and take him into his room. He kisses drunkenly, sloppily. I try to sway his inebriation into passion. His dick hangs limp. I try to work it. I try it for quite a while. I am determined to win, but it is useless. I am useless. Still, it is decided that we will go to prom together. Tom would never go back to his alma mater's prom, even if he were allowed to, and Darren, at 22, isn't interested either. So, since Ramon is single now, why not?

Of course, Ramon winds up getting back together with his girlfriend the day of the prom. He sits across the limo from me and barely says a word the whole time. They smoke pot incessantly. It is my prom, I think, I should splurge. Enjoy myself. Sure…let me hit that.

Every inhalation brings me deeper within myself, within my own dread. The music is ominous and the conversation frightens me in its drug-centricity. I walk into the prom to see all these strangers. This isn't how prom is supposed to be. This is not a celebration of the time we'd all spent together, sharing myriad memories from childhood on. I don't know these people at all. They don't know me. The teachers who are there as chaperones do know me, and they know of my recent troubles. I am sure that they know I am high now. There is little to question as I emerge red-eyed from the limo that holds the school's A-list burnouts. They all leave me alone when we get inside. I sit mostly alone. I dance mostly alone. I don't care what they are doing afterward, I've had enough. They drop me off in the apartment complex. Alone. Mom doesn't have a chance to ask whether I'd gotten high, I am too busy crying about how awful it had been.

I go back to NA and sit in the crowd. As we all introduce ourselves, I'm this person and I'm an addict, I start to cry again. I have to turn in my one-month sober key chain. I've relapsed. "I'm Jaime, and I'm coming back," I say. That's what you say if you are returning after a relapse. How furious these people must be with me. They've had their relapses in alleys, people wondering where they are and fearing them dead for weeks, months, years. I was at my prom. I had three hits of a joint in a limo. I am coming back, I say. I nod my head gravely, tears streaming from my eyes. Am I mourning my lapse or my rejection at the hands of my prom-party peers? You'd think I had gotten used to the latter sort of thing.

SEVENTY-FIVE

I still foster the most ridiculous hope that I can return to Mac Arthur to attend their prom, preferably with Mark Lanzer. Nobody asks. Nobody even calls, ever. It is like I had never been there at all. Maybe I hadn't.

I am sure that, away from the pressures of our high school social system, Mark would love me. I want to give him that opportunity. I call him. We talk for a little while. I tell him that I am taking my new friends to the surfer beach near our old neighborhood and ask if he wants to come along. "You made friends?" he asks, incredulously. It stings. Is that so hard to believe? It seems more an earnest query than attack though, so I am not dissuaded. I tell him I have, stopping just short of telling him that I had gone to the prom with the guy voted cutest in the class, thank you very much. I am not the type to brag or qualify myself, except, perhaps, in these pages. Whenever I do, the guilt outweighs the glory. Besides, I think my remark would be disqualified by the fact that the "cutest" didn't touch or talk to me for the entirety of the evening.

Still, he says he will go! Mark Lanzer is going to hang out with me! He is going to go to the beach with me, Cheyenne and Lana. I am so excited, but coolly, coooolly. I will pick him up the next day at noon.

Mom lets me borrow her car. I drive to Levittown, showing my cute new friends my ugly old neighborhood. My heart races as we wind our way to Mark's house. I am cool, I am cool, I will be fine. I am cool. The door is closed when we get there. I pull into the driveway, not noticing the car parked out front. I approach the door. I am cool, I am cool, I am cool. I ring the doorbell.

Mark's mother answers the door. I presume it is his mother, as I've never met her. I beam my highest watt smile at her, "Hi, I'm Jaime, I'm here for Mark?" I say. She looks confused. She tells me he isn't there. I don't cry. For once I don't cry. My jaw tenses. No mother likes her son to be an asshole. "Oh," I say. "We had plans. He told me to pick him up." "I'm sorry," she says. "It's okay," I say coolly, I am cool, I am cool. "I think he owes me an apology, though." I turn to get back into the car, my new friends looking on with incredulous confusion. I hear doors slam. That's when I notice the car at the curb.

From it pours Charlie Beltram and his buddies, a collection of those who had been cruelest to me through the years. They lean against their car, looking at me. It seems they are there to watch and enjoy my humiliation. "Hey guys," I say tensely, with a smirk. I get back in my car. The girls ask what happened. "He made a total asshole out of me," I say. I almost laugh as the tears dance behind my eyes. "What a dick," they exclaim. Yeah. "Yeah...what a dick," I reply, but I don't know if I am talking about him or myself. I don't make a scene though, for once I don't make a scene. And I hope the guys noticed how hot my friends are and how cool I am now, and I hope that they will tell Mark and that they will all feel stupid and cruel. I hope that, but I know they will probably just laugh.

SEVENTY-SIX

I graduate. Just barely, but I do. Strings were pulled, concessions were made. I wasn't passing, but come on, I had been an honor student. I can't get left back in my senior year. Hardship is plead, circumstances considered. I'd had to move, I'd gone crazy...there are all sorts of factors at play. I slide under the radar. As they call my name to accept my diploma, there is only a handful of applause. That great popularity meter of graduations and awards ceremony death lists has failed me. Nobody knows who I am. I've just gotten there. Who? Jaime Andrews? We went to school with a Jaime Andrews? You can hear the question echoing in the dearth of slapping palms.

My grandparents and aunt come back to the apartment to share a cake. I am glowing with pride and sobriety. I am done. I've gotten through. Done are all those days of sitting at tiny desks, staring down at the fragile wrists that, with one swift action would spare me a seemingly endless procession of days. I don't have to do it anymore. It is over and I am okay.

I am more than okay. I am going to be great. I'm going to college to be an actor. I get a car. Finally, my own car, as much a reward for my graduation as for my new drug-free lifestyle. My mom was holding some of my early savings for me, wisely, and I chip in the entirety of it, paying for half of this eight-year old car. Dad goes with me to buy it. It's really cute. A Dodge Colt, apparently driven by an old lady, back and forth to church or something. In eight years, it had accrued only 30,000 miles. It's silver and grey. We take pictures from the apartment balcony with me splayed on its hood. Everything is great.

I have a job. It's only for the summer, but I will be working the grand opening of Old Navy, the bastion of mass-produced blandness. I volunteer to dress and form the dummies in the children's department. They are creepy, malleable, headless dolls with sticks jutting out of their necks on which hats can be perched. I am as happy to be doing something creative as I am angry that I'm not compensated for it. Most of the time I have to stand around in the aisles, smilingly offering help to people that don't want or need it. I feel useless and annoying. Every person I greet takes a piece of me with them on their search for bargain jeans and tees. The soundtrack of pop confections is designed to be unobtrusive, but manages to burrow into my mind further with each turn on its two-hour rotation. We won't get a new mix for another month. I don't know if I can make it.

I don't know why life seems so oppressive to me. Why it always has. Why every day is such a trial for me when everyone else appears to get along fine. Without the buffer of pot, my days return to their previous intensity. My thoughts race unintelligibly, making me dizzy. I begin seeing yet another therapist. Someone at her job had recommended him to my mother. I wonder what the people my mother work with think of me, how much she has disclosed to them. They must think I am crazy. I guess I am.

As I disclose my litany of troubles and their ephemeral origin, I cry about my still persistent urinary tract infections. The doctor asks where it hurts, which seems obvious to me, but I shove my hand to my urethra, weepingly obliging. I tell him that it isn't because of sex, because this has been going on since I was seven years old. I don't know from where I pluck that age. I have a generally pretty awful sense of time, and that's just what pops into my head. The air in the room contracts. "What happened to you when you were seven years old?" he asks. "I don't know," I howl. We are out of time. I feel like a breakthrough has been made, though. All of those years of therapy and finally, someone is acknowledging that something had, in fact, happened to me. I must be covering up something in my memory to protect myself, but at last, a doctor believes there is a reason, a genesis for my anger and ill feeling. I feel like if only I could know the origin of my pain, I could finally move past it. I don't go back the following week though. The next day, it's all over the news that an area shrink has been busted making sexual advances on his adolescent patients. He was having a relationship with one of them. It is my shrink.

Damn. I was finally getting somewhere, too. Or maybe I wasn't. He had made me point at my own crotch, after all. Maybe supporting theories of abuse was his way of getting close to young, confused women. I'm not an idiot, though, he had to know that. I wouldn't fall for a creepy old predator. I am needy, but not that pathetically so. I think.

I want to get high again. Just to see if I can. Just to see what will happen. What is the big deal of just doing it on occasion? Eryn is still home for summer break. I miss Eryn. I miss getting high with Eryn. She is going to drive out to visit me.

We walk through a local park and sit on a rock outcropping of a small, mossy lake. She packs her bowl and we pass it back and forth. She asks if I noticed it's a new bowl. I hadn't. She talks about it in detail, pointing out the chambers and the markings. It freaks me out. I don't want to talk about it. I want to enjoy it and discuss other things, I want to relax. Talking about it makes it sordid. We are in these woods, hiding out, doing drugs. I have to leave. This isn't fun anymore.

That doesn't stop me from giving it another chance, though. I'm not ready to give up just yet. I go up to visit my college for an orientation. My mom drove me, but the parents and prospective students are staying in different dorms. Everyone is broken into different groups and will present a lip-synched song at an assembly the next night. Fate decrees that there will be only one man in our group, and - commandeering as ever - I decide our song should be "The Tide is High," by Blondie. Everyone agrees and we, or I, proceed to choreograph it. No one argues or bristles. It makes sense: I am there as an acting student, we are putting on a performance. I make an effort not to make myself central in the production, but when showtime comes, there I am center stage, hamming it up while the other girls cluster uncomfortably together. It is a competition, and those are something I loathe to lose, but I have to hand it to the next group. They hang their heads backwards over chairs with shirts taped under their mouths and eyes drawn on their chin. They sang "The Lion Sleeps Tonight." It's hysterical. There is no contest. We come in second. I am fine with that. I can always demur in the face of superiority.

I gravitate toward a group huddled together in the back of the presentation room. They are those of unkempt hair and intense stares, less crisply dressed, wearing fatigues or baggy jeans and band t-shirts. These are my people. My people are going out to the parking lot to get high later. This is how you make friends.

They knock on my door and I walk with them across the road to the mostly empty parking lot. The three of them had driven down together, sans parental unit, from further upstate. I get into the backseat with the other girl. We crack our windows and the driver puts Pink Floyd on his stereo. "Dark Side of the Moon." Insanely enough, I've never heard it and I admit this to my fellow passengers. "Oh, you're shitting me, man," says the driver, "just listen."

"Just listen." The words come at me ominously through the smoke as he turns the volume dial up. Every time I exhale, the music deepens. It's just like my bad acid trips. I release some breath and, each time, the music darkens in concert with my exhalation. I feel as though my lost breath cannot be reclaimed, and that if I allow the song to play out, it will result in the eventual elimination of all air from my body. I try to talk myself out of it. I will be fine. I've felt like these horrible things are going to happen before, and nothing ever does. I try to make light of it. "Man, I'm bugging out," I say, as casually as I can. "Yeah, this music's nuts, right?" says the girl to my right. The driver turns around to face us. "Yeah...or it could be the DRUGS." Everyone else laughs, but my head swoons with the horror of it. I have to get out.

I throw open the door and burst into the fresh air, breathing it in. I can still hear the music. My head is heavy and I have to sit. "I'm sorry," I say, "can you put on something else?" The driver obliges as he steps out of the car to see what my problem is. I hang my head between my knees, focusing on the ground. "I just can't smoke pot anymore, I guess." I feel like an asshole. I don't want to ruin anyone's good time. They must think I am such a big freak. A little girl that can't handle some fucking pot. When my head finally stops spinning, I walk back to the dorm by myself. This is not how you make friends.

It's for the best though, right? I don't need friends like that. I'm not going to smoke pot anymore. I have to make new kinds of friends. I hear that there is a recovery floor for non-users in one dorm, maybe I can live there. Maybe I should. Maybe then I would be okay.

I will be okay.